ABOUT THE AUTHOR

Called "One of the People to Watch in 2003," Maria Shaw is a professional astrologer, intuitive, and author. She is a columnist for *Soap Opera Digest* and *Tigerbeat* magazines. Maria has appeared on *FOX News*, *Mr. Personality*, *The Anna Nicole Show*, and *Soap Talk*. Her national tour and lecture schedule takes her all across the United States. A former model and television news anchor, Maria hosts a weekly radio program.

Maria Shaw's STAR GAZER

YOUR SOUL SEARCHING, DREAM SEEKING, MAKE SOMETHING HAPPEN GUIDE TO THE FUTURE

2003
Llewellyn Publications
St. Paul, Minnesota 55164-0383, U.S.A.

First Edition
First Printing, 2003

Book design and editing by Joanna Willis
Cover illustration © 2002 by Digital Vision/PictureQuest
Cover design by Gavin Dayton Duffy
Illustrations on pages xvii–xviii, 2–4, 9, 14, 19, 24, 29, 33, 38, 43, 47, 51, 55, 59–60, 62, 79, 81–92, 94, 103, 106, 109–110, 113–114, 117–118, 120–121, 123, 125–126, 128–129, 214, 216–228, 230–234, 240, 242–258, 260–282, 284–303, 315–317 © 2003 by Svetlana Chmakova
Other interior illustrations by Llewellyn art department
Universal Tarot cards by Roberto De Angelis © 2000 are reprinted with permission from Lo Scarabeo

Library of Congress Cataloging-in-Publication Data
Shaw, Maria, 1963–
    Maria Shaw's star gazer: your soul searching, dream seeking, make something happen guide to the future.—1st ed.
        p.   cm.
    Includes bibliographical references and index.
    ISBN 0-7387-0422-9
        1. Occultism—Juvenile literature. [1. Occultism. 2. Fortune telling.
3. Astrology. 4. Numerology.] I. Title.

BF1411.S52 2003
133—dc21
                                                                                    2003051661

Llewellyn Publications
A Division of Llewellyn Worldwide, Ltd.
P.O. Box 64383, Dept. 0-7387-0422-9
St. Paul, MN 55164-0383, U.S.A.
www.llewellyn.com

 Printed in the United States of America on recycled paper

To Jana and Sierra

CONTENTS

ACKNOWLEDGMENTS

Special thanks to my family and friends and all of those associated with Maria Shaw & Company over the years. Also much appreciation goes to my publicists Steve Allen and Jarrett Morgan. Thanks to all of my wonderful clients, supporters, and the great team at Llewellyn, especially Megan and Lisa.

INTRODUCTION

There are thousands of New Age books on the market these days. Lots of information about astrology to spirituality to developing your own intuition is readily available. But are they really New Age or "new thought"? Think about it: many of these ancient arts and sciences have been around for centuries, only to disappear or go underground depending on the religious or governmental tone of the nation. Just within the past thirty years "New Age" has become more accepted in mainstream society. Lots of folks get their tarot cards read. People have begun replacing an old way of thinking about spirituality with a "new thought." Think how lucky you are to live in a day and age when you're free and encouraged to develop your spiritual and intuitive gifts. Just as recently as the 1970s, any New Age theory was considered taboo and you didn't find many books written on the subject. Now, thanks to the younger generation and those searching for a higher truth, astrology, numerology, palmistry, and many of the New Age arts are being studied, taught, and enjoyed by millions of people. Many your age are searching for spiritual truths, thirsty for ancient knowledge and getting in touch with their higher self.

You've heard the words *psychic* and *intuitive*. We all are sensitive, intuitive beings. We all have these special gifts. Intuition is easier to discover and develop than one might think. If you, too, have been searching for a way to connect with your higher self and discover your intuitive side, congratulations! You are on a wonderful journey of growth and discovery. Finding this book is part of that journey. In this manual, designed especially for teenagers, you'll find everything you've ever wanted to know about you! Learn astrology by reading about your sun sign. If you've always wondered what those lines in your palm meant, read on! There's a beginner lesson on how to read the sacred tarot deck, as well as a guide on dreams and their interpretations. If numerology (the study of numbers) fascinates you, I've included a guide to discover your birth number and what it personally means for you. Look for an in-depth chapter on auras and the meaning of color, as well as a crystal guide. You'll learn how easy it is to create real magic with the candle-burning section.

There's an old saying: "When the student is ready, the teacher appears." You're ready since you picked up this book! You are about to begin a personal journey, filled with answers to a lot of questions you may have been asking yourself. Enjoy the trip!

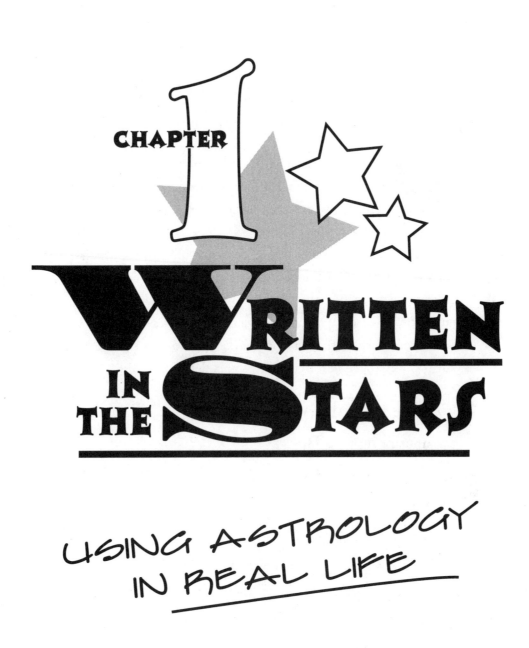

CHAPTER 1

Written in the Stars

USING ASTROLOGY IN REAL LIFE

Wouldn't it be wonderful if you could be psychic for a day? When you first meet someone, you can size him up and know exactly what kind of person he is: his likes, dislikes . . . his personality?

Well, it's easier than you think. Just knowing someone's birthday can give you the inside scoop. There are specific personality traits associated with each of the twelve signs of the zodiac. Find your sun sign below. (These dates change by a day or two from year to year, so if you were born at the very beginning or end of a sign, check the year you were born in for your sun sign's dates.):

Aries: March 21–April 20

Taurus: April 21–May 21

Gemini: May 22–June 21

Cancer: June 22–July 22

Leo: July 23–August 22

Virgo: August 23–September 23

Libra: September 24–October 22

Scorpio: October 23–November 21

Sagittarius: November 22–December 22

Capricorn: December 23–January 20

Aquarius: January 21–February 19

Pisces: February 20–March 20

Some signs get along very well together, while others just don't seem to connect. Look around you. Who are your friends? When are their birthdays? Chances are, you and your close pals all have compatible sun signs. What about the girl or guy you've had your eye on? Could a relationship develop? Will he or she find you attractive too?

Understanding even a little bit about astrology and the traits associated with each sign will help answer some of these questions. You'll have fun learning more about yourself too.

This chapter is devoted to the twelve sun signs of the zodiac. Besides reading about your own lucky number and day of the week, you'll find fascinating facts about each sign's personality. You'll learn about friendship and dating compatibility.

There's another piece of information you may find interesting in this chapter: a section on decans. Each zodiac sign is divided into three periods called *decans*. For example, there is a first decan Cancer, a second, and a third. Your decan corresponds to the ten-day period in which you were born. Each produces a different influence over the personality. Read more about your own decan and its characteristics at the end of each section.

So, you're off to a good start! Discover your special talents and traits. Look up your best friend's sign. Then check out that special someone you've had your eye on!

You'll gain a whole new understanding of the people in your school, perhaps on the job, and in your social circle. You'll amaze your friends with your newfound knowledge!

THE ARIES TEEN

March 21–April 20

Symbol: The Ram

Color: Red

Ruling Planet: Mars

Element: Fire

Gemstone: Diamond

Lucky Day: Tuesday

Number: 9

Aries teens are full of fire! The fire signs—Aries, Leo, and Sagittar-ius—are ambitious, self-driven, and confident. Yet Aries are also described as "bossy." What they truly are are born leaders.

Being the first sign of the zodiac, Aries is the pioneer of the group. Your friends who are born under the symbol of the Ram enjoy initiat-ing projects. They like to tell people what to do and how to do it!

The key phrase for Aries is "I am." Many feel the world centers around them. They are bright, funny, intelligent, and have a lot of energy.

Aries teens can be broken down into two categories: the Brains and the Flirts!

The Brains are known for being very smart and many rise to the top of their class, spearheading activities and being involved in stu-dent government. There are a great number who make the honor roll. These kids plot a career path before graduation and practice their valedictorian speech long before they start their senior year.

Just as many, however, fall into the second category: the fun-loving Flirts! These guys and dolls love to exchange flirtatious glances, pass love notes back and forth, and often kiss and tell! Aries gals can't wait until the Sadie Hawkins dance every fall. They can finally take the lead and ask the object of their affection out! The Aries guys love to know there's a girl in every class admiring them.

If you're dating an Aries or have your eye on one, here's a word of warning: this sign loves the chase! They are only as good as their last conquest. The harder you are to catch, the more interested they are. So go ahead and flirt outrageously, but don't agree to their every whim. They'll lose interest fast.

Aries love the idea of being in love. They fall hard and fast. Be cau-tious: in September they may plead undying devotion, but by Hal-loween they're trick-or-treating with someone new. Guys born under the sign of the Ram like to date older girls, so it's not unusual for a sophomore to have his eye on the senior homecoming queen. He may even harbor a secret crush for the home economics teacher!

Aries' most compatible love signs are Sagittarius, Leo, Gemini, Aquarius, and Libra. Good friends can be found among fellow fire signs as well as Pisces and Taurus. There'll be squabbles with Scorpio, Capricorn, and Cancer.

Because Aries are so full of energy, many enjoy playing sports and are fine athletes and team captains. Their competitive nature and desire to be number one can lead their teams to first-place victories, but they sulk if they go unrecognized. All feel the MVP honor should be theirs!

As a friend, Aries teens are great fun to hang out with. You'll never be bored! They hate being bored, so they are always conjuring up things to do on the spur of the moment. Sometimes they think before they act, but they have a tendency to get grounded more than other signs because of their impulsive actions. They are also known for being lead-foots. Their driving record makes for lively conversation!

Aries is a sign that doesn't like authority, although they respect it. Remember, they enjoy bossing others around. So regular tiffs and arguments with parents are just part of being an Aries teenager.

Once Aries set their sights on a goal, they are excited about achieving it and can create great things. The power of their mind is strong. Because of their optimistic nature, it is important that Aries are surrounded by positive people. Negative naysayers can drag them down. They need to claim their own identity during their teenage years. If nurtured, this can be one of the most productive and successful periods of their life.

THE ARIES DECANS

FIRST DECAN ARIES

March 21–March 30: You are a true Aries. You are ambitious, enthusiastic, and have lots of energy. There's nothing you can't do. You'll try anything once.

SECOND DECAN ARIES

March 31–April 9: You have many qualities of the Aries born in the first decan, but add creative abilities to the list. You will always be "young at heart" and have a good sense of humor.

THIRD DECAN ARIES

April 10–April 20: You could strike it rich someday! You're always at the right place at the right time. Lady Luck will shine brightly upon you.

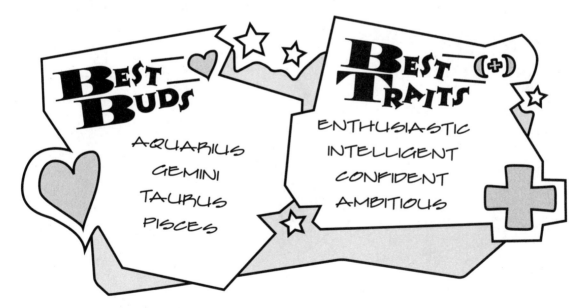

BEST BUDS

AQUARIUS
GEMINI
TAURUS
PISCES

BEST TRAITS

ENTHUSIASTIC
INTELLIGENT
CONFIDENT
AMBITIOUS

Aries

Amazing Attractions

SAGITTARIUS
LEO
LIBRA

Worst Traits (-)

IMPATIENT
SELF-CENTERED
RECKLESS
BOSSY

Heart-Breakers

CANCER
CAPRICORN
SCORPIO

Careers to Consider

TEACHER
ARCHITECT
PSYCHOLOGIST
SUPERVISOR
POLICE OFFICER
COACH

THE TAURUS TEEN

April 21–May 21

Symbol: The Bull

Color: Green

Ruling Planet: Venus

Element: Earth

Gemstone: Emerald

Lucky Day: Friday

Number: 6

Loyal, steadfast, dependable, and stubborn—three out of four ain't bad! These are all adjectives used regularly to describe the Taurus personality.

Taurus folks, in general, are salt-of the-earth-type people. Taurus teens are usually laid back with easy-going personalities—until they lose patience. It takes a lot to get a Taurus mad, but when you do, watch out! You'll find yourself dealing with a raging bull in a china shop.

Taurus are known for being bull-headed. Once they have set a goal, it's as if they have tunnel vision—nothing will stand in their way. No matter how long and hard the road before them may lay, Taurus will go the extra mile to achieve their goal.

Most Taurus teens want to land a job as soon as they can legally work. This is not because they necessarily like to work, but because they want to make their own dough. Taurus is notoriously known as the money monger of the zodiac. Remember the kid selling drug-store candy on the school bus? Probably a Taurus. But if not careful, Taurus could eat up their profit. Taurus teens enjoy food: tacos, burgers, French fries, desserts, you name it. Taurus love to eat, so it's important that they stay active in sports or gym class so as not to put on excess weight.

Taurus teens are either really lazy or very ambitious. There is no in-between. They are either on the run all of the time—working, dating, filling up their social calendar—or they just sit in front of the boob tube with a bag of Doritos.

What motivates a Taurus? A goal that's not easily attainable. Tell a Taurus teen she can't do something and she'll go all out to prove you wrong—especially if there's a reward, say in the form of cash, at the finish line.

Young Taurus need security and a solid home base more than other signs, with the exception of Cancer. A loving, stable family is important.

Bulls are possessive of their things and must have space in the house to call their own. Having to share a room with a sibling is a disaster as Taurus don't want anyone touching their personal belongings. They tend to accumulate lots of stuff. Many refuse to part with ragged stuffed animals and broken toys aging in the corner closet. A decent car to drive is also a must. No rundown jalopy that grandpa traded in past its prime will do.

In friendships, Taurus have a small circle of close pals who enjoy the same interests. Because of their stamina, Taurus guys are involved in sports like football, weightlifting, and wrestling. These guys like to annoy and tease the girls they're interested in before asking them out. Taurus of both sexes show no interest in the loud, life-of-the-party types. When Taurus teens decide to date, they usually pick gentle, attractive, and stable companions. They don't put up with phonies or show-offs.

Relationships with Taurus are usually long-term and could stretch over a period of years. Even if the object of their affection is dating someone else, Taurus will patiently wait until the person is free. They won't settle for anything less than their heart's desire. It may take Taurus a while to ask someone out or even accept a date, but once they do, they consider a relationship serious business. They expect a lot of attention, affection, and honesty. Dating two people at one time is unusual and likely frowned upon. It's their loyalty and dependability that help create long-lasting relationships.

Cancer, Capricorn, Virgo, and Pisces are traditionally strong love matches for the Bull. Leo and Aquarius prove more difficult. Aries, Gemini, and Libra make good buddies. Scorpio is Taurus's opposite sign and although there is physical attraction between the two, it may take patience and tact to make a long-lasting union.

Taurus teens, for the most part, don't give their parents a hard time. The truly stubborn ones do, but the discipline and maturity many show often lead mom and dad to think their teenager is a pretty good kid.

Their best subject is math—probably because they like to count money so much!

Taurus will find their teenage years enjoyable if they have a structured environment and stable home life. A daily routine and schedule works best for them. They are patient and hard workers if they have a goal and loyal and trusted friends.

THE TAURUS DECANS

FIRST DECAN TAURUS

April 21–April 29: You will find luck in love and the pleasures that life has to offer. You could be artistic or musically inclined.

SECOND DECAN TAURUS

April 30–May 9: You will be logical, down-to-earth, and not as emotional as first decans. Your business, money-making, and organizational skills are topnotch.

THIRD DECAN TAURUS

May 10–May 21: You are the most serious of all Taurus. Nothing gets past you. You can be more stubborn and focused than your counterparts.

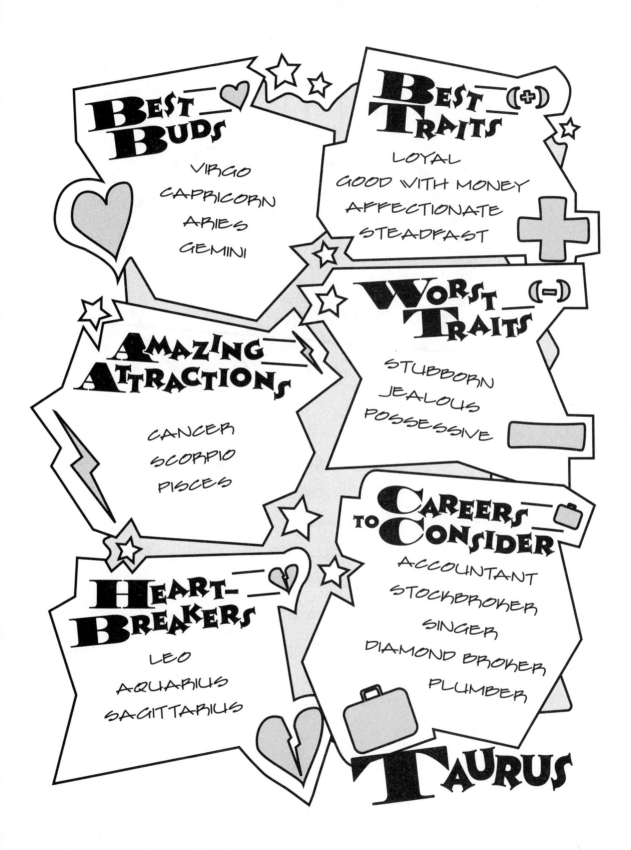

BEST BUDS

VIRGO
CAPRICORN
ARIES
GEMINI

BEST TRAITS (+)

LOYAL
GOOD WITH MONEY
AFFECTIONATE
STEADFAST

AMAZING ATTRACTIONS

CANCER
SCORPIO
PISCES

WORST TRAITS (-)

STUBBORN
JEALOUS
POSSESSIVE

HEART-BREAKERS

LEO
AQUARIUS
SAGITTARIUS

CAREERS TO CONSIDER

ACCOUNTANT
STOCKBROKER
SINGER
DIAMOND BROKER
PLUMBER

TAURUS

THE GEMINI TEEN

May 22–June 21

Symbol: The Twins

Color: Yellow

Ruling Planet: Mercury

Element: Air

Gemstone: Pearl

Lucky Day: Wednesday

Number: 5

Living with a Gemini is similar to having two roommates. Gemini is the sign of the Twins, and many teen Twins admit they feel like Dr. Jekyll and Mr. Hyde sometimes!

Ever hear of the good and evil twin theory? Those familiar with Gemini know all about it. That's why kids born in late May and June can seem sweet as syrup one minute, and in the next be the darnedest little devil you've ever had to deal with!

At least they're very versatile! In fact, Gemini thrive when busy. They get bored easily, so variety is the spice of life.

Gemini are known for their communication skills too. They talk all of the time. Cell phones are attached to their lips. Gemini usually have a personal phone line installed in their room by age thirteen.

You'll find many Gemini on the forensic or debate teams, hosting school radio programs, and entering creative writing contests. If they're not enjoying the latest bit of gossip, they're passing notes to their buds during an algebra test.

Gemini are smart, but if not challenged, they lose interest and their grades may not always reflect their true academic abilities. Sometimes socializing gets in the way of attaining high grades, but if time is well managed, they can certainly handle it all.

Gemini adore animals and little kids and often themselves look younger than they are. Forget about lying about your age Gemini—you'll get busted every time! And speaking of stretching the truth, Gemini are good at that. They make the best storytellers. Their creative minds are constantly ticking.

In relationships, Gemini are looking for fun. A good sense of humor helps. They don't want a boyfriend or girlfriend who is smothering and around all of the time, but they do need someone who will talk a little and listen a lot. Some are fickle with friendships and love affairs. Because they enjoy change, the Twins are open to trying new things. They get bored with people easily and tire of the same old routine.

Rather than hanging out with just one friend, Gemini like to do things in groups. Both guys and girls have lots of friends of the opposite sex. Gemini girls feel just as comfortable with their boy "friends" as they do with their gal pals.

Aquarius, Libra, Aries, and Leo are favorable love matches for the Twins. Cancer and Taurus are among those called friends. Pisces and Virgo may clash. Sagittarius is their opposite sign and usually makes for an interesting and lively relationship.

The Twin girls like to try new fads and usually sport the latest fashions; they are constantly changing their hairstyles and make-up. The Gemini guy has some sort of creative ability, but often keeps it a secret. Only closest friends or family know of the beautiful poetry he writes or the detailed drawings found on his sketch pad. They're deep thinkers too. Both sexes can put on a fun-loving, ditsy act, but beneath the surface is a probing and intelligent soul.

Most Gemini enjoy school. They like to learn as much as they enjoy socializing. The communication skills they develop in teenage years are put to good use as many become teachers, public relations experts, salespeople, and entrepreneurs.

Many Gemini teens often do not know what they want to do when they grow up and are ambivalent about their indecisiveness. They shouldn't be! Most born under this zodiac sign take time to enjoy life. They are not in a hurry to grow old, but live in the moment. In fact, many Twins reach a peak in their fifties and enjoy great success. Their lives will never be boring—they won't stand for it!

FIRST DECAN GEMINI

May 22–May 31: Your mind is very strong and can easily see both sides of a coin. You combine logic with creativity.

SECOND DECAN GEMINI

June 1–June 11: You can be very romantic and write the best love letters! You believe you'll marry your soul mate one day.

THIRD DECAN GEMINI

June 12–June 21: Sometimes you feel like a loner. You are a very deep person with great wisdom and creative gifts to share. Learn to take more risks!

BEST BUDS

LIBRA
AQUARIUS
GEMINI
CANCER

BEST TRAITS

COMMUNICATIVE
CREATIVE
SOCIABLE
VERSATILE
YOUTHFUL

Gemini

Amazing Attractions

SAGITTARIUS

ARIES

LEO

Worst Traits (—)

DEVIOUS

RESTLESS

TWO-FACED

DECEPTIVE

Careers to Consider

TEACHER

JOURNALIST

LIBRARIAN

WRITER

TRAVEL AGENT

Heart-Breakers

PISCES

VIRGO

CAPRICORN

SCORPIO

THE CANCER TEEN

June 22–July 22

Symbol: The Crab

Color: Silver

Ruling Planet: The Moon

Element: Water

Gemstone: Moonstone

Lucky Day: Tuesday

Number: 9

Cancers are the most sentimental of all the zodiac signs. These are the people who save every little memento. They have a "memory box" stashed in their bedroom closet filled with photos of kindergarten classmates, seventh-grade love letters, and a frayed friendship bracelet. They keep everything, including their dearest friends.

Make a Cancer friend in high school and it's a good bet you'll be doing lunch twenty years later, or swapping grandbaby pictures in fifty.

This is a sign that doesn't let go—of the good times and the bad. If you hurt a Cancer's feelings and thought all was forgotten, you'll be mistaken when the class reunion rolls around. Likewise if you cheered one on during a difficult period—this sign will be indebted to you forever.

Cancer teens are very sensitive—even the guys—but you wouldn't know it. They have a cool, calm exterior. But deep below the Crab's hard shell, their feelings and self-confidence can suffer a great deal.

They are bright, funny, caring, and a little bossy of their friends. Sometimes mom is their best friend. Cancers can be ambitious, but they are not threatening or pushy.

Cancers are very good at manipulating others. If they don't get their way one way, they will step back and go about getting their needs met from another angle.

Cancer girls are usually very feminine. Although modest, some like to show their great figures off. They fall madly in love and are very romantic. Their emotions run so deep that even after a relationship has ended, they can hang on to unrequited love for years.

Cancers are attracted to the guys that are "full of fire," and often idolize someone that doesn't belong on a pedestal. Scared of rejection and being hurt, it's not likely a Cancer girl will ask a guy out. She will be traditional and wait—impatiently—for him to ask her.

The Cancer males are often called "the nice guys." They make their girlfriends feel so protected and cared for. These are the young men that open the car door for you on a date, take flowers to your mother, and buy you teddy bears. They like the shy, respectable girls to bring home to mother. Cancers of both sexes are highly influenced by mom's opinion.

Taurus, Virgo, Scorpio, Pisces, and other Cancers bode well for love. Capricorn is the opposite sign, which means a strong attraction, but sometimes this match can prove to be difficult. The Goats are logical, while the Crabs are highly emotional. Cancers have harder times with Aries and Libra in romantic relationships, but these signs can be super friends. Aquarius is a no-go.

Cancers are known to be moody. Any little slight or rude remark will push them to tears. The guys keep everything inside, and the girls will cry at the drop of a hat.

However, Cancers are generally good kids. If they grow up in a negative environment, some have emotional problems that take years to work through. They keep walls up. They don't trust anyone or let anyone get too close to them. But if they are raised in a safe, secure, and happy home, Cancer teens are self-assured. They thrive and become successful, ambitious, and giving people. Many do volunteer work and are involved in traditional groups like scouting and 4-H.

Cancer teens want people to think well of them, especially their parents. They love their family and are good with younger siblings. Most do well in school and have a close circle of friends.

Cancer is also one of the most intuitive signs. They are born with strong psychic antennas and feel things deep in the pit of their stomachs. They are sympathetic to others. If a classmate is being harassed or teased, it's usually a Cancer who goes out of her way to offer sympathy to the victim. They may not always stand up to a bully, but Cancers will make the wounded feel better in some way.

At times, Cancers get crabby. They try not to, but they can't help it. Their moods swing depending on the course of their ruling planet, the Moon. Full moons can really affect them emotionally.

Self-confidence plays a big role in a Cancer's mood and self-image. If they are well liked at school and among their peer group, they will remember their school days as one of the best times of their lives. If they didn't feel accepted—whether it be real or imagined—they can hang on to the pain of rejection for years. But it sometimes drives them to do great things and become successful. There are more self-made millionaires born under the sign of Cancer than any other sign.

Cancers' true happiness, whether they be fifteen or fifty, will always be their home and family. That includes friends they consider family. They are the mothers and fathers of the zodiac; the gentle and protective souls that love from the bottom of their hearts.

THE CANCER DECANS

FIRST DECAN CANCER

June 22–July 2: You are the most psychic of all Cancers. You have great intuitive powers, are very caring and nurturing, but can be insecure.

SECOND DECAN CANCER

July 3–July 12: You love a good mystery. You can't stand it if someone has a secret, but you're sure good at keeping one! You'd make a great detective.

THIRD DECAN CANCER

July 13–July 22: You are the most sensitive of all the Cancers. You exude an aura of glamour and class.

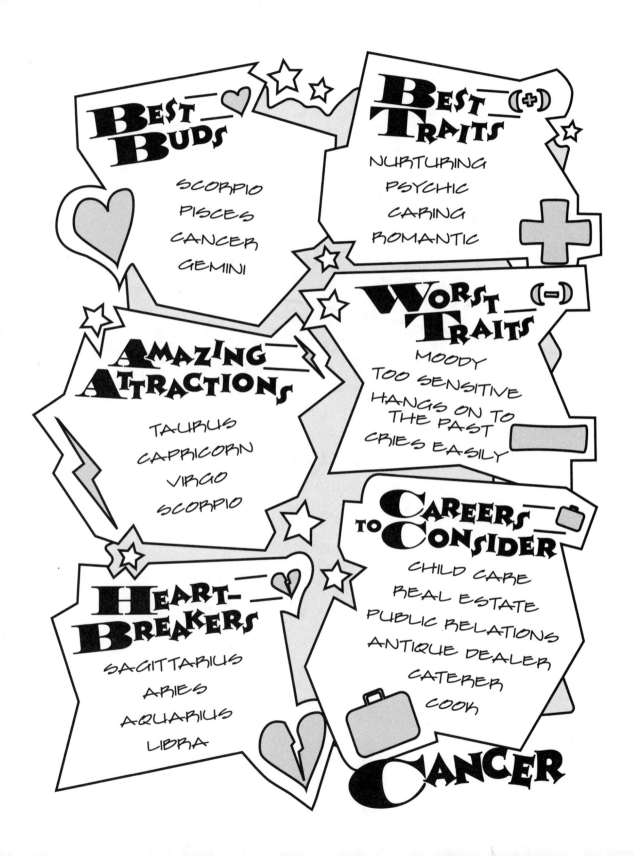

Best Buds

SCORPIO
PISCES
CANCER
GEMINI

Best Traits (+)

NURTURING
PSYCHIC
CARING
ROMANTIC

Worst Traits (-)

MOODY
TOO SENSITIVE
HANGS ON TO THE PAST
CRIES EASILY

Amazing Attractions

TAURUS
CAPRICORN
VIRGO
SCORPIO

Careers to Consider

CHILD CARE
REAL ESTATE
PUBLIC RELATIONS
ANTIQUE DEALER
CATERER
COOK

Heart-Breakers

SAGITTARIUS
ARIES
AQUARIUS
LIBRA

CANCER

THE LEO TEEN

July 23–August 22

Symbol: The Lion

Color: Orange

Ruling Planet: The Sun

Element: Fire

Gemstone: Ruby

Lucky Day: Sunday

Number: 1

The Leo teenager will grab the spotlight—or at least let it shine on him for a while. These summer-born babies love to be adored, admired, and noticed. After all, they are the kings and queens of all the zodiac. Just about everything that Leos do they do in big, dramatic fashion.

You will find many Leos carrying lead roles in school plays. The drama plays out in their everyday lives too—they create chaos. Many Leos play the role of the class clown. They are born entertainers, whether it be in the lunchroom or theater class.

Leos are generous to their friends, but they need to be appreciated and thanked for good deeds. In love, they wear their hearts on their sleeves. Even when they suffer a bruised ego or a broken heart, Leos jump back into the dating game.

The Leo guys love to have beautiful women hanging on their arm. They especially like the tall blondes or model-type brunettes. The Leo girls want to be treated like royalty and expect their dates to lavish them with attention and gifts. They usually go for the jocks or those in the popular clique. Good looks are mandatory. They want to be number one in their boyfriend's life and will not settle for anything less. If a guy shows them disrespect or embarrasses them in any way, he's snubbed immediately. In love, Leos want it all and expect to get it.

Sagittarius, Libra, Gemini, and Aries make for fun dates. Leo is the sign of royalty and its opposite sign is Aquarius, which rules the "common man." Leos can learn a great deal about relationships from the Water Bearer. Taurus and Scorpio challenge the Leo, but Cancer and Virgo prove to be supportive friends.

Leos are known for their big egos. They enjoy being flattered and told just how wonderful they are, but they do know the difference between hogwash and true admiration. They are great leaders and attract many followers. President Bill Clinton was born under the sign of Leo. Leo teenagers start school trends, and you'll find one usually sits at the head of the lunchroom table (their royal throne).

Leos strive to be the best at everything because they have such a strong sense of pride. It's important to find a balance in their lives. If they enjoy the social scene too much, Leos may have to work harder at academics. They are creative and are often found taking art and mass media as elective classes.

Leos care what other people think of them. Their reputation and appearance are very important. They are fussy about their hair. The lion's mane has to be perfect. Many have been known to be late for school because of a "bad hair day." The Lionesses have a strong sense of fashion and like the "notice me" type of clothing. Both sexes like jewelry, especially anything gold.

Lions are anxious to find employment and many are promoted to assistant manager positions while still in high school. They love to work and make money. The paychecks don't always go into a college fund; money is spent at the mall. This sign loves to shop. Leos have been known to lavish gifts on people they care about as well as themselves.

Leos also love to throw parties. Socializing is part of the daily routine. Being the "life of the party" comes naturally.

Many Leos are class presidents, team captains, and pep rally leaders. They have a strong sense of school spirit and enthusiasm. They are loyal friends, but if hurt or rejected, they can turn and walk away from a long-term connection.

Their leadership and people skills will help Leos get ahead. Many graduate from high school and go right into college or start a business.

Most Lions get their fifteen minutes of fame and then some. Their talents and charisma shine, but it's the generosity of their spirit and heart that help Leos make their biggest contributions to the world.

FIRST DECAN LEO

July 23–August 1: A star is born! You would make a great entertainer. You have charisma and a winning personality.

SECOND DECAN LEO

August 2–August 12: You tend to be more easy-going than other Leos. You are funny, witty, and lucky!

THIRD DECAN LEO

August 13–August 22: You enjoy being pampered and made over. You like to initiate new projects and are always up for a challenge.

Best Buds

ARIES
SAGITTARIUS
CANCER

Best Traits

GENEROUS
LOVING
LOYAL
LEADER

Leo

Amazing Attractions

AQUARIUS

LIBRA

GEMINI

Worst Traits

ARROGANT

EGOTISTICAL

WORKAHOLIC

BOSSY

Heart-Breakers

TAURUS

SCORPIO

CAPRICORN

Careers to Consider

HOTEL OR RESTAURANT MANAGER

BUSINESS OWNER

ACTOR

AGENT

THE VIRGO TEEN

August 23–September 23

Symbol: The Virgin

Color: Blue

Ruling Planet: Mercury

Element: Earth

Gemstone: Sapphire

Lucky Day: Wednesday

Number: 5

Virgos are here to serve others. They need to be needed. That's why you'll find so many born under this sign in helping fields or involved in some sort of service work. Virgo teens take great pride in an ability to organize things and help out wherever they can. Here you'll find the student office aides, church youth volunteers, and prom clean-up crew.

For all of their hard work, Virgos seldom get applause, but they do feel a sense of satisfaction for a job well done.

Virgo is one of the most dependable signs of all the zodiac. Virgo teens hate to be late for anything. In fact, most arrive early wherever they go.

Virgos want everything to be perfect. They can be their own worst critic and strive to be the best at everything they do. If they do not meet their own expectations, they get depressed.

"Perfect" means their sense of style too. Even in younger years, Virgos are choosy about their "look." They are not as flashy as Leos or as flamboyant as Aries, but their style is classic. Their shoes, socks, and yes, even underwear, must coordinate. The girls are fussy about make-up, and a single hair out of place drives them mad. The guys usually opt for the preppy or clean-cut look.

Virgos are just as fussy about the food they eat. Many are into health and nutrition programs, diets, and workouts.

Perhaps Virgos' best quality is also their worst: the ability to analyze deeply. These teens will worry and pick things apart until their stomach gets upset. But their analytical mind serves them wonderfully in classes such as science and math. They can get to the root of a problem like no other.

In love, Virgos are particular, and once they make a commitment, they usually don't stray. They expect the same from their partners. Some are shy and seem hard to get to know. Many people mistake Virgos' shyness for a snobbish attitude, but that's not usually the case. The Virgo is just covering up an insecure feeling with an air of aloofness. Both sexes don't buy into pick-up lines. They want honest communication. Virgo girls have been known to be late bloomers in the dating arena; some go for months turning down dates.

Taurus, Capricorn, Cancer, and Scorpio are solid choices for love. Sexual experimentation usually begins later than most peers, hence the "Virgo the Virgin" jokes. Sagittarius, Gemini, Aries, and Aquarius may not appeal to a Virgo. Friends are meant to be kept for years and are considered just as close as family.

As a student, it is not unusual for those born in late August and September to be exceptionally bright. Many are interested in health and science careers after graduation. Virgos make great doctors and health-care professionals. Some excel in owning a service-oriented business. They usually know exactly what they want to be when they "grow up."

Virgos' gift to society is their ability to unselfishly give of their talents to others. However, they need to remember that even though they are such wonderful givers, it's important they learn to receive as well!

THE VIRGO DECANS

FIRST DECAN VIRGO

August 23–September 1: These are often the most critical of all Virgos. You are extremely sharp. You are quick-witted and full of life.

SECOND DECAN VIRGO

September 2–September 11: You are ambitious and driven. You find it hard to deceive or lie. Honesty is your policy. You are mature for your age.

THIRD DECAN VIRGO

September 12–September 23: These are the affectionate Virgos. You like to cuddle and kiss. You can be very romantic and creative too.

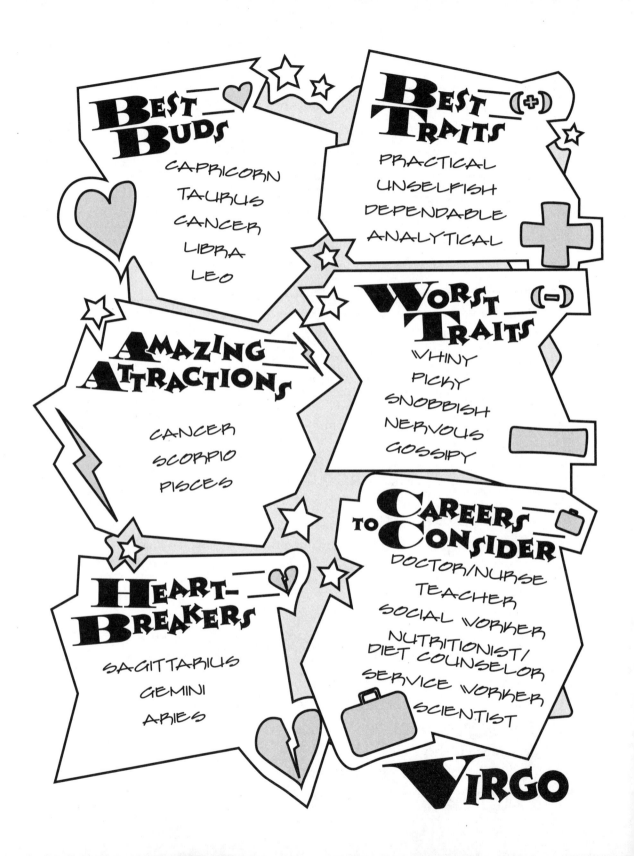

Best Buds ♥

CAPRICORN
TAURUS
CANCER
LIBRA
LEO

Best Traits ⊕

PRACTICAL
UNSELFISH
DEPENDABLE
ANALYTICAL

Amazing Attractions

CANCER
SCORPIO
PISCES

Worst Traits ⊖

WHINY
PICKY
SNOBBISH
NERVOUS
GOSSIPY

Heart-Breakers ♥

SAGITTARIUS
GEMINI
ARIES

Careers to Consider

DOCTOR/NURSE
TEACHER
SOCIAL WORKER
NUTRITIONIST/
DIET COUNSELOR
SERVICE WORKER
SCIENTIST

VIRGO

THE LIBRA TEEN

September 24–October 22

Symbol: The Scales

Color: Pink

Ruling Planet: Venus

Element: Air

Gemstone: Opal

Lucky Day: Friday

Number: 6

Ruled by the planet Venus, Libra teenagers are naturally charming and considered attractive. They are well liked by many of their peers and tend to be social butterflies.

Libras have lots of friends and few enemies—partly because they try to get along with everyone. Libras hate confrontation and arguments. They love parties, flirting, and good gossip. Many Libras play the role of matchmaker for friends and are quite good at it!

Romantic, creative, and very friendly, Libras are the first to welcome a newcomer to the neighborhood or school.

Regarding relationships, Libras like to be in them. They don't like going solo. It's hard to find a single one, and when they do break from a love affair, they're not single for long! Libra was put on this planet to learn about love and relationships. They fantasize about their wedding day years before they walk down the aisle. Life brings them many love lessons, but they never give up, and they believe wholeheartedly in the theory of soul mates.

Some Libra guys, however, can be very picky when deciding whom to ask out. They have a vision of Miss America planted firmly in their mind. She sits high on a pedestal, and very few come close to this ideal. It would be better if Mr. Libra would lighten up a little. A bit of imperfection can make a person interesting! So, these lover boys miss out on relationship opportunities with great potential because their expectations are too high.

Libras can be very easy-going though. In fact, sometimes they can be so easy-going that it frustrates their friends to no end. It's okay to fight back once in a while. It's fun to make up! But Libra despise arguing, so they just give in a lot.

The other thing that drives their friends crazy is they can't make up their mind. Ordering a pizza takes forever. What do you want on it? Don't ask a Libra. They'll change their minds a dozen times and then finally ask, "What are you going to have?" They weigh everything before making a decision. Remember their symbol is the scales.

Libra doesn't like to be alone. Have you ever noticed how the Libra girl always asks her friend to tag along to the powder room? She feels more comfortable in pairs or in groups.

Since love is so important, Libras need to make good choices for mates. Cancer and Capricorn won't do, but Aries, Leo, Gemini, and Sagittarius may be long-lasting matches. It's important that their partners approve of their friends and not be the jealous type. He or she needs to be exciting, romantic, and someone who knows how to order a good pizza.

Most Libras go through a party period in their teen and early adult years. This eventually wears thin. It's like a phase of their life that needs to be experienced. As they grow up, Libras tend to settle down nicely, still enjoying a social scene, but not one wild party after another.

All in all, Libras are gentle, kind-spirited teenagers who really don't give their parents too much trouble. Some should consider becoming lawyers since Libra rules law and they can be very fair and diplomatic. They are the peacekeepers of the zodiac and their peace-loving ways will bring comfort to those around them.

THE LIBRA DECANS

FIRST DECAN LIBRA

September 24–October 3: You are the most romantic and creative of all Libras. You strive for peace, harmony, and balance in your everyday life.

SECOND DECAN LIBRA

October 4–October 13: Life will never be boring! You are the social butterfly. Your calendar will be full. You tend to be a bit of a rebel.

THIRD DECAN LIBRA

October 14–October 22: Given a gift for gab, you love to talk. You're good at manipulating (in a nice way), so you get your way a lot!

BEST BUDS

GEMINI
AQUARIUS
VIRGO

BEST TRAITS

FAIR
GOOD-LOOKING
FRIENDLY

LIBRA

AMAZING ATTRACTIONS

ARIES
LEO
SAGITTARIUS

WORST TRAITS (-)

INDECISIVE
JUDGMENTAL
MOODY
ALOOF

HEART-BREAKERS

CAPRICORN
CANCER
SCORPIO
TAURUS

CAREERS TO CONSIDER

LAWYER
ARTIST
MATCHMAKER
MUSICIAN
MARRIAGE COUNSELOR
DIPLOMAT

THE SCORPIO TEEN

October 23–November 21

Symbol: The Scorpion and the Eagle

Color: Black, burgundy

Ruling Planet: Pluto

Element: Water

Gemstone: Topaz

Lucky Day: Tuesday

Number: 9

Scorpio is the most powerful sign of the zodiac. Those born under the symbol of the scorpion have the ability to create their own destiny. They have more determination, control, and willpower than any of the other signs, including Leo and Taurus. But you wouldn't know it—sometimes Scorpios appear very laid-back as if they wouldn't hurt a fly. Beneath a cool facade lies an intense, strong presence. If a Scorpio really believes in something, he will get his way, one way or another—sometimes even to his own detriment!

Scorpios are psychic creatures. They love studying the occult, getting tarot readings, and playing with the Ouija board.

Many Scorpions have the ability to communicate with deceased loved ones either though dreams or sensing a presence in their energy field. Since the planet Pluto, which rules death (breaking down and rebuilding), is the ruling planet of Scorpio, those born in late October and November often have strong feelings about the afterlife.

When younger, many Scorpios may have "visits" from loved ones who cross over. These "imaginary friends" try to connect with family members left behind. Children are naturally psychic and quite open, so the souls of the departed find it easy to communicate with them.

In the everyday world, Scorpios are good at manipulating things to their benefit. They have a way of getting their way. Some are overachievers; nothing will stop them on the way to the top.

Scorpios are emotionally intense and when they feel, they feel very deeply, but they seldom express these thoughts. They can be obsessive if infatuated with something or someone, and hang on to lost love for years. They never forget an enemy either!

In relationships, Scorpios need to have control. They want to do the dumping or breaking up. Others find them attractive, and Scorpios are known for having lots of sex appeal. It's their hypnotic eyes that get you hooked every time! There's something about those deep, intense eyes that make you feel as if the Scorpio is reading your mind!

When in love, Scorpios can be loyal but jealous, affectionate but secretive. You'll never know exactly what Scorpios are thinking. They like to keep secrets, but they can't stand it if you have one. Want to drive your Scorpio friends crazy? Let them know you have some juicy gossip but can't tell a soul. They'll be at their wits' end trying to pry bits and pieces of information from you—and they'll probably get it!

The Scorpio guys can be possessive and jealous, but the girls got them beat! Mess with their boyfriend and beware the consequences!

The Scorpio guy is known for stealing peeks in the Victoria's Secret catalog, while his female counterpart experiments with lipstick and make-up at an early age.

Taurus is Scorpio's opposite sign. These two will find each other stimulating and attractive, but both can be hotheaded and like to have their way. Cancer and Pisces are well suited to the Scorpion personality, as is Capricorn and Virgo. Leo and Aquarius relationships don't stand a chance.

You'll find Scorpios on the honor roll and excelling in sports, for they love competition. They enjoy science too. Because of their deep, probing minds, they make excellent private detectives. Natural healing abilities make them great doctors and psychologists.

Scorpios can be respected leaders as long as they don't turn into dictators and go after a position of power for the sake of power. Their ability to get through a crisis and rise above obstacles is their greatest gift. They can do anything they set their strong minds to. This is one sign that can change the world!

THE SCORPIO DECANS

FIRST DECAN SCORPIO

October 23–November 1: Your drive and ambition are greater than most. You can be very intense and emotional. Attaining power and wealth is important to you.

SECOND DECAN SCORPIO

November 2–November 11: You can be dreamy and romantic. You have a great imagination. Be careful of being too paranoid about things. You smell evil even when there is none.

THIRD DECAN SCORPIO

November 12–November 21: You could have many trust issues. Be more open to others emotionally. You have the ability to create wealth and prosperity in your life.

BEST BUDS

CANCER
PISCES
SCORPIO
LIBRA

BEST TRAITS

DEVOTED
STRONG
INTUITIVE
LOYAL

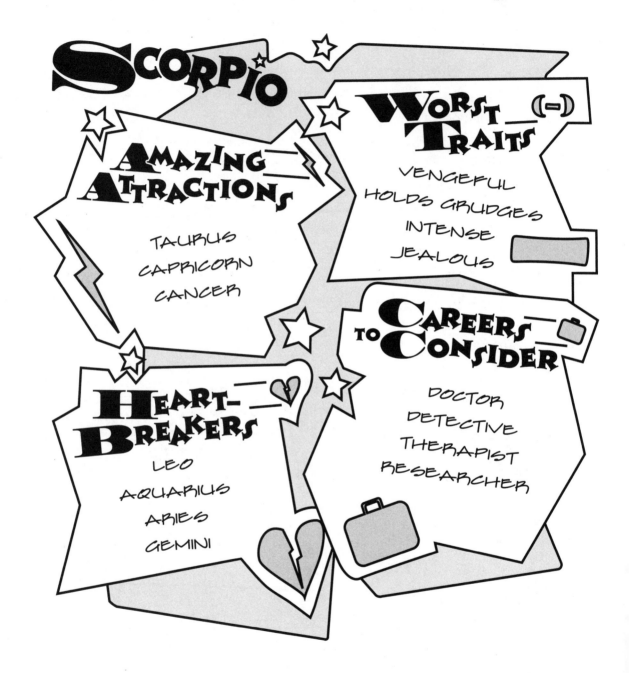

Scorpio

Amazing Attractions

TAURUS

CAPRICORN

CANCER

Worst Traits (-)

VENGEFUL

HOLDS GRUDGES

INTENSE

JEALOUS

Heart-Breakers

LEO

AQUARIUS

ARIES

GEMINI

Careers to Consider

DOCTOR

DETECTIVE

THERAPIST

RESEARCHER

THE SAGITTARIUS TEEN

November 22–December 22

Symbol: The Archer

Color: Purple

Ruling Planet: Jupiter

Element: Fire

Gemstone: Turquoise

Lucky Day: Thursday

Number: 3

Sagittarius is ruled by the lucky planet Jupiter. It's no wonder those born under this sign always seem to land on their feet. They have extra protection and a guardian angel hovering over their shoulder. Sagittarius tend to be upbeat and positive too. They play the role of counselor to friends, but hate to burden others with their personal problems.

If you want an honest answer, ask a Sag. They don't feel right about lying to anyone. They are direct. They are blunt. They will tell you exactly what they think. Be prepared for the truth.

Many Sagittarians love to travel. Without wheels, the Archer feels confined and imprisoned. Sag teens are the first to sign up for driver's education. They tend to be social creatures, enjoying lots of friends, school activities, and sports. There are many athletes born under this sign. Sagittarians have a natural athletic ability.

Sagittarians are likable and charming. This is the fellow that can get away with cutting class, or at least talk his way out of a detention slip every now and then.

In relationships, Sagittarians are hard to tie down. They don't like commitment. There are too many fish in the sea! If you want a real challenge, set your sights on a Sagittarius man. They like adventurous girlfriends who can double as a best buddy. They have no problems with dating more than one girl at a time.

The Sag girls are the outdoorsy types. They are sexy in a down-to-earth sort of way. Fun to hang out with, these gals are great talkers and often popular with their classmates. They don't have the reputation for being players like their male counterparts, but they can hold their own in relationships.

Sagittarius' best love bets are Aries, Leo, Libra, and Gemini. Stay away from emotional Cancer, Pisces, and Virgo. Aquarius and Scorpio are fun to hang out with.

Besides enjoying a busy social circle, Sag's interests include history, foreign culture, and religion. A thirst for higher knowledge is insatiable. They love to debate things and usually win their arguments.

Spiritual growth also plays a big role in Sagittarius' lives. They search to uncover their soul's purpose and the secrets of the universe.

Many born under this sign yearn to be world travelers and will become airline pilots and flight attendants. Others are found teaching in large universities, owning businesses, working in real estate or interior design.

The Archers are overly optimistic at times and believe everything will work out for the best. Life is a glorious adventure with new opportunities around every bend. These are the people who can't wait to see what the next day holds in store.

Sagittarius' greatest strength comes from their strong desire to seek out the truth, to build a strong spiritual self, and share positive energy with everyone they meet.

THE SAGITTARIUS DECANS

FIRST DECAN SAGITTARIUS

November 22–December 1: You are the luckiest of all Sagittarius. You are a quick learner. You will travel the world over.

SECOND DECAN SAGITTARIUS

December 2–December 11: You are honest and direct. Energy levels run high and you'll have many interests.

THIRD DECAN SAGITTARIUS

December 12–December 22: Your personality shines the brightest. Everyone loves being around you! You have a way with words and are truly a charmer!

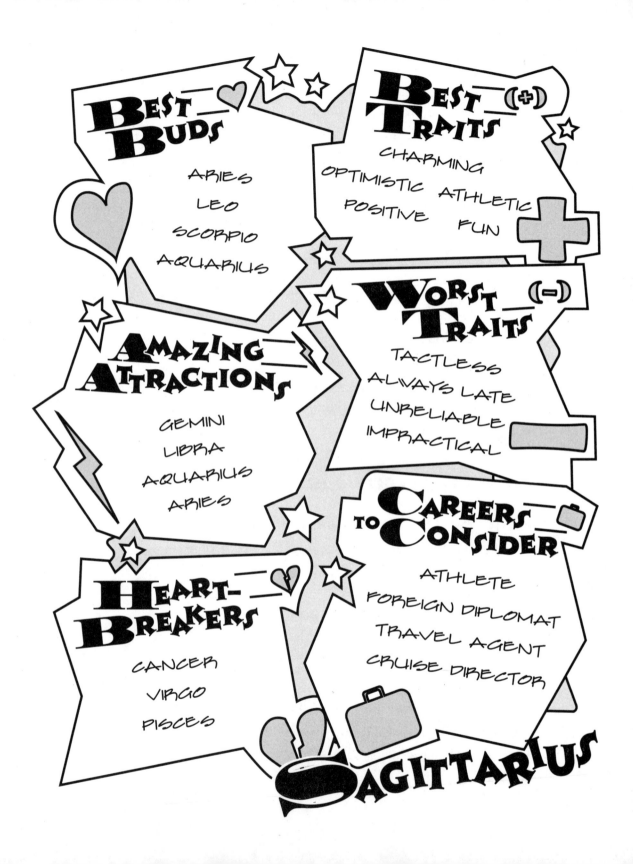

Best Buds

ARIES
LEO
SCORPIO
AQUARIUS

Best Traits ((+))

CHARMING
OPTIMISTIC   ATHLETIC
POSITIVE   FUN

Worst Traits ((-))

TACTLESS
ALWAYS LATE
UNRELIABLE
IMPRACTICAL

Amazing Attractions

GEMINI
LIBRA
AQUARIUS
ARIES

Careers to Consider

ATHLETE
FOREIGN DIPLOMAT
TRAVEL AGENT
CRUISE DIRECTOR

Heart-Breakers

CANCER
VIRGO
PISCES

Sagittarius

THE CAPRICORN TEEN

December 23–January 20

Symbol: The Goat

Color: Black, silver

Ruling Planet: Saturn

Element: Earth

Gemstone: Garnet

Lucky Day: Saturday

Number: 8

Capricorns are old when they're young and young when they're old! This sign ages in the opposite direction. Capricorn youngsters are mature, organized, and wise for their years. When they reach age forty, they often try to establish the childhood they never had. A midlife crisis can create rash decisions and major havoc in their stable lives.

As young adults, Capricorn teens have a grown-up demeanor. They are cautious and dependable. They are apt to keep their rooms tidy and in order and get their homework done ahead of schedule.

Capricorns love tradition and respect their elders. Family history and genealogy interest them—and so does the business world. Even at a young age the Cappys are mapping out career paths and learning about money and investments. Unlike other signs, Capricorn kids usually put some of their allowance in the bank.

Goat kids are cautious in love. They fear being rejected, but you'd never know it. Beneath a cool exterior is a sensitive guy or girl. The guys are dubbed the strong, silent types and are very masculine. They expect to play the traditional role of asking a girl out for a date, opening her car door, and paying for dinner.

The Capricorn girl is classy and unpretentious. She tends to be serious-minded and very smart. She isn't apt to get lost in daydreams or fantasy. Logical and down-to-earth, she expects her dating partners to be gentlemen. Capricorns could find their soul mates among the Taurus, Scorpios, Cancers, and Virgos. Leave Aries, Geminis, and Libras alone.

Most Capricorn teenagers enjoy working, but are serious about education first and foremost. They recognize that college or additional training is needed to get ahead in today's world and usually pursue higher study. They set sights on careers that pay well, and are in high-demand fields such as business, medicine, and teaching.

These teens care a great deal about their reputation and take steps to safeguard it. Good grades are important, but famous-brand clothing is too! Ask any Capricorn girl what designer names are hot. She'll give you the lowdown. Even though social status and looking good is important, Cappys don't enjoy being in the spotlight. They prefer to be the power behind the scenes.

Whether it's debating current events or arguing about a Saturday night curfew with parents, Capricorns won't back down on a topic they believe in. No wonder they are called the Goats of the zodiac!

Capricorns' gift to the universe is their wisdom and logic. They have great ability to create a new future while keeping the traditions of the past alive.

THE CAPRICORN DECANS

FIRST DECAN CAPRICORN

December 23–December 31: You are the most serious-minded of all Capricorns. Keeping a positive outlook is important for your self-confidence and success.

SECOND DECAN CAPRICORN

January 1–January 10: For those born under this decan, you have a creative flair and a romantic edge like no other. Members of the opposite sex find you very attractive.

THIRD DECAN CAPRICORN

January 11–January 20: You have terrific communication skills and can talk to anyone. You relate well to people of all ages. Loosen up a little in love. Learn to take some risks. You'll be pleasantly surprised.

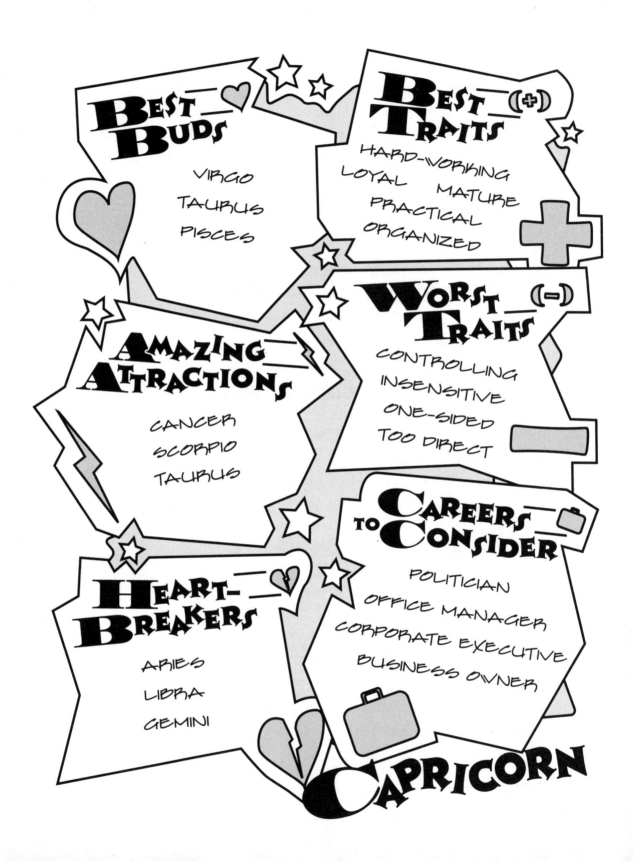

BEST BUDS

VIRGO

TAURUS

PISCES

BEST TRAITS (+)

HARD-WORKING

LOYAL   MATURE

PRACTICAL

ORGANIZED

AMAZING ATTRACTIONS

CANCER

SCORPIO

TAURUS

WORST TRAITS (-)

CONTROLLING

INSENSITIVE

ONE-SIDED

TOO DIRECT

CAREERS TO CONSIDER

POLITICIAN

OFFICE MANAGER

CORPORATE EXECUTIVE

BUSINESS OWNER

HEART-BREAKERS

ARIES

LIBRA

GEMINI

CAPRICORN

THE AQUARIUS TEEN

January 21–February 19

Symbol: The Water Bearer

Colors: The rainbow

Ruling Planet: Uranus

Element: Air

Gemstone: Amethyst

Lucky Day: Saturday

Number: 4

Those born under the sign of Aquarius are truly unique individuals. They do not follow the crowd. The Water Bearer sets high standards and creates a style all his own.

These are the humanitarians of the zodiac. They believe in social causes. You'll find some active in politics, student government, and youth group council.

Aquarius' motivation is to create change. They hope to make the world a better place, whether it be in their neighborhood, school, or society as a whole. Most are adamantly opposed to any sort of discrimination and social injustice.

Some Aquarius are loners and highly intellectual. Almost all show an interest in computers and new technology. They enjoy sporting the latest gadgets and gizmos.

Aquarius friendships are extremely important. Many make friends their "family." They don't feel bound by traditional family ties. By age eighteen, they are ready to cut the apron strings and leave home for new adventures.

Aquarius sometimes confuse their admirers because they treat them like buddies. They don't get mushy with affection. In fact, they can appear cool and detached, but don't mistake that for not caring. Aquarius do care and deeply, but they don't wear their hearts on their sleeves. They usually date in groups, and go through many personal ups and downs in relationships. Since personal freedom is such a big issue with this sign, a possessive steady won't last long in an Aquarius's book.

Leo, their opposite sign, can make for good company. Sagittarius, Gemini, Libra, and Aries are also good matches for the Water Bearer. But the fire cools down quick with a Cancer, Scorpio, or Taurus.

Aquarius kids like to sport the latest fashion trends; that includes the "shock me" look. These kids are among the first to dye their hair purple, get tattooed, and pierce body parts. At the very least, they wear some of the coolest clothes in the crowd. Anything that makes them "different" matters. Often they are years ahead of their generation because of imaginative thinking and trend-setting ways.

Although they work well in new technology fields, Aquarius also have a talent for working with animals. Do you know Aquarius is one of the few signs that opt not to have kids when they get older? Some do, but many surround themselves with beloved pets. Aquarius make great vets. Other career choices include research, police work, and the military.

Aquarius, like Aries, is the sign of the know-it-all. They can speak on almost any subject and enjoy entertaining friends with crazy stories.

Sometimes Aquarius feel as if they don't fit in and are often misjudged by parents and peers. The close friends Aquarius make usually are friends for life. They prefer socializing in groups rather than one-on-one. They will fight for causes, against injustices, and against prejudice.

Since they possess such an undying devotion to something or someone they believe in, it's not a bad idea to have an Aquarius on your side!

THE AQUARIUS DECANS

FIRST DECAN AQUARIUS

January 21–January 29: Some may call you a genius. You may find yourself in unique and unusual careers. You are also good at inventing things.

SECOND DECAN AQUARIUS

January 30–February 8: Your friends are very important to you. You go out of your way to help others, and work great in team efforts.

THIRD DECAN AQUARIUS

February 9–February 19: You tend to be less of a rebel than others born under your sign. Peace and love are your mottos. You can be affectionate and playful.

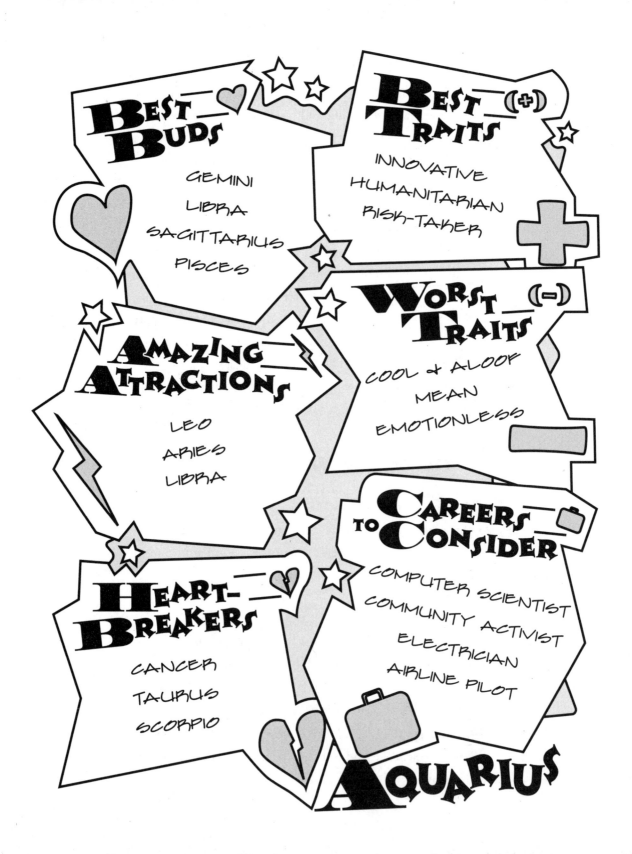

THE PISCES TEEN

February 20–March 20

Symbol: The Fish

Color: Blue

Ruling Planet: Neptune

Element: Water

Gemstone: Aquamarine

Lucky Day: Thursday

Number: 7

These are the big dreamers of the zodiac. Pisces, also referred to as the Fish, are lovable creatures who aim to please. They want everyone to like them and often go out of their way to win approval. Sometimes they feel guilty over the smallest slights.

Yes, Pisces tend to be very sensitive and wear their hearts on their sleeve.

Pisces' eyes are usually their best feature. They are beautiful and sparkling, just like the sea. The Fish can be romantic and imaginative. A favorite pastime is daydreaming.

Pisces is also one of the psychic signs. Their strong intuitive powers help them ride the roller coaster of life. This sign seems to have more than their share of bumps in the road. I often joke there are more Pisces guests on *Jerry Springer* than any other sign!

Life for Pisces is never simple. They really do live a soap opera. Maybe they draw chaos to them because of their giving and gullible nature. It is often a Pisces child who begs to keep a lost puppy or nurse the sick kitty.

As a friend, Pisces are kind and supportive and enjoy gossip just as much as their Gemini peers. Because they are so sensitive, Pisces are like a sponge—they soak up everything around them. They are a product of their environment. If there are happy people in their home, Pisces are happy. If they are caught in a family war zone, they fall into pity parties like no other.

You'll find many born under this sign interested in the occult and psychic experiences. They have strange and bizarre dreams and are encouraged to keep a dream journal. If Pisces can learn to interpret their dreams, they can gain much wisdom and insight into the future.

In love, Pisces are romantic but can be smothering. Cancer, Scorpio, Taurus, Capricorn, and their opposite sign, Virgo, are good matches. Aquarius and Gemini are better left for friends. A Sagittarius match is inadvisable.

Pisces, like the Cancers, can hang on to lost love for years. So they need to find stable, down-to-earth types to date. Unfortunately, they usually choose people who have a little too much "fire." Pisces girls are attracted to the "bad" boys. The Fish men like girls who will allow them to be a knight in shining armor. Both sexes play the role of the martyr well.

Some have to guard against a tendency to use escapism as a way to release tension or stress. They should avoid drug and alcohol use. Pisces is influenced by peer pressure more than any of the other signs. Their need for acceptance is strong.

Psychology, art, and drama are all classes Pisces can excel in. They are born actors and have a natural gift to make people smile and cry, sometimes at the same time. Pisces will touch your heart like no other, work hard to please, and make sure your life is happy. They may even teach you to daydream. Getting lost in a fantasy isn't always bad, now is it?

THE PISCES DECANS

FIRST DECAN PISCES

February 20–February 28: You are artistic and romantic. You can get lost in your daydreams easily. Keep your feet on the ground.

SECOND DECAN PISCES

March 1–March 10: You are compassionate and very caring. You aim to please. Sometimes you can be moody, but you have great intuitive gifts.

THIRD DECAN PISCES

March 11–March 20: Spirituality and its teachings hold great interest for you. Your life's goal is to help save the world!

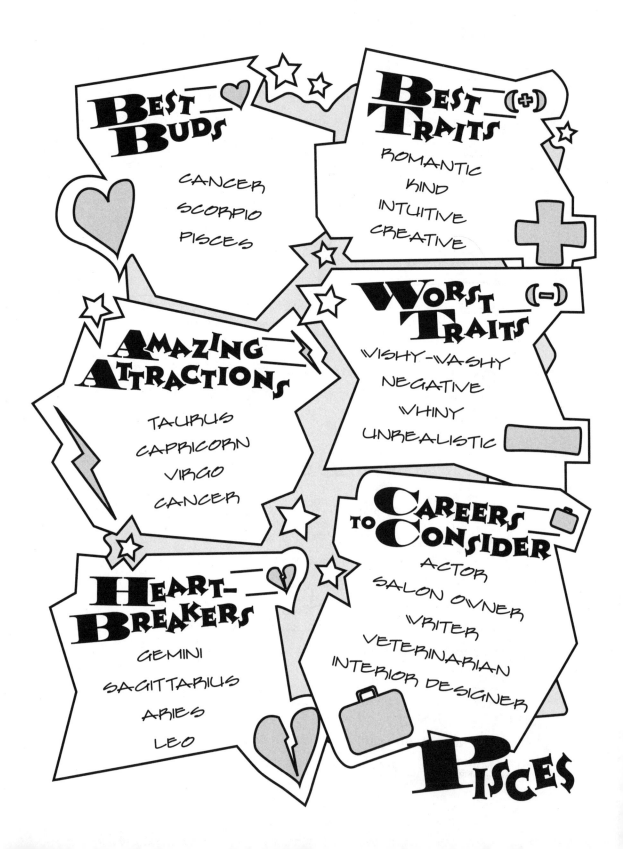

Best Buds

CANCER

SCORPIO

PISCES

Best Traits ((+))

ROMANTIC

KIND

INTUITIVE

CREATIVE

Amazing Attractions

TAURUS

CAPRICORN

VIRGO

CANCER

Worst Traits ((-))

WISHY-WASHY

NEGATIVE

WHINY

UNREALISTIC

Heart-Breakers

GEMINI

SAGITTARIUS

ARIES

LEO

Careers to Consider

ACTOR

SALON OWNER

WRITER

VETERINARIAN

INTERIOR DESIGNER

PISCES

Here are the morning Announcements

WRITE YOUR THOUGHTS ABOUT
ASTROLOGY HERE!

I hope you enjoyed that piece!
Happy B-day to Amanda Crocker
on Doris Chiu, todays super
visors at recess is Mrs Craig
and Mrs Janzen Lunche Super
visors are Mr McEachern
and Mrs Harding. Todays library
supervision is Shirley yen
and Grace Chun, Garbage
duty is div.1 please try to
keep our area clean! thank
you for your work this
week !!!

59

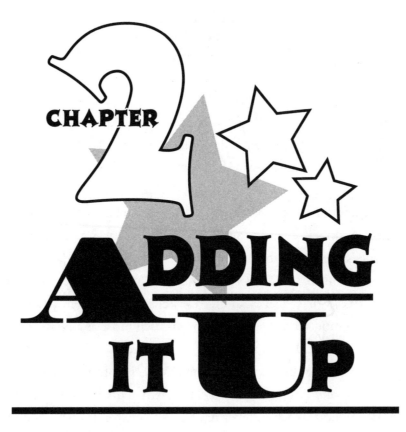

CHAPTER 2

Adding It Up

NUMEROLOGY AND YOU

I s the day you were born considered lucky or cursed? Do the numbers in your birth date add up to success? *Numerology*, the study of numbers, can shed some light on your personality traits and your life path.

Numbers have power. Your sports team chants "We're number one!" Number seven is considered lucky. Unlucky thirteen is to be avoided. Heaven forbid if the thirteenth falls on a Friday! Over the course of history and for thousands of years, the ancient science of numerology has been taught, researched, and taken seriously by many. In modern times, numerology is used more as a New Age tool.

If you can add, you, too, can learn numerology.

We can trace the origins of numerology back to the Greek mathematicians and philosophers from the sixth century B.C.E. According to their studies, each number has a personality of its own. Odd numbers have stronger energy than others and a more powerful vibration. They are regarded as masculine numbers. Even numbers carry less strength and are said to be feminine. Why are odd numbers stronger? Because when you add odd numbers to even, the result is always an odd number.

Mystics and philosophers also believed the human psyche is already determined at birth and can be divided into nine stereotypes of the primary numbers one to nine. This is where the basic birth number system many numerologists use today came from. The formula is easy to learn. You'll be amazed at how accurate it is.

How to Determine Your Birth Number

The process is simple. Write out the day, month, and year in which you were born. For example, if you were born on October 12, 1985, you would write down the number like this:

$$10/12/1985$$

Then add the numbers together in three separate parts (month, date, and the year). Example:

Month: $1 + 0 = 1$ Day: $1 + 2 = 3$

Year: $1 + 9 + 8 + 5 = 23$

Now add the three totals together: $1 + 3 + 23 = 27$

You want to reduce the final number down to a single digit of 9 or less:

$$27 \text{ is } 2 + 7 = 9$$

So the birth number for someone born on October 12, 1985 is the number 9.

This next paragraph is important. There are two numbers that are very special numbers. They are called *master numbers*. They are explained in the last part of this chapter. If your final number happens to add up to 11 or 22, do not reduce it to a single digit. These are the only two numbers you do not reduce. People born with these birth numbers have special purposes, which will be explained later.

BIRTH NUMBERS

NUMBER ONE

Number One people are leaders. They are independent, fiery, and have great organizational abilities. They usually have strong minds. As young adults, they are not always at the top of the class, but they are gifted in some way. Number Ones need to be the "best" at something. They are competitive and expect to win. They want to be noticed, adored, and loved.

In their teen years, Number Ones enjoy hanging out with adults rather than kids their own age. They are more mature than most peers. Some are known to marry fairly young and have troubled relationships. It is best for Number Ones to wait until they're older to settle down. They can be self-centered and overachievers, leaving little time and attention for their mates.

Number Ones think they can "have it all" and will do their best to get ahead in life—many times they do. If you are a Number One teen, consider yourself lucky; you'll have a lot of enthusiasm for life and won't take no for an answer. You surely won't settle for being number two! In your heart, you know you are special. You recognize you deserve great things and you work hard to make them happen. Just don't be too critical and impatient with others who may not see things your way. You can be mature for your years, but you don't know everything—just not yet!

The nice thing about Number Ones is that they have a great ability to take charge and get things done. If you're a Number One and your friend is having trouble with her parents, you'll offer sound advice. If a student committee needs a chairperson, you're up for the job. You have a lot of confidence and energy. Why shouldn't people believe in you? Everyone looks to you for leadership. That's why many Ones are popular at school or respected on the job. They don't wait for things to happen. They make things happen! That's one of the biggest differences between you and some of your friends—you are an "achiever." You will let nothing stand in your way. Some people may call you ruthless, cocky, and even arrogant. Don't let them bother you. You know you have what it takes to succeed! Go after your dreams!

Famous Number Ones: Halle Berry, Reese Witherspoon, Charlize Theron, and Martin Luther King, Jr.

NUMBER TWO

If you're a Number Two, "compassionate," "caring," and "loving" would best describe you. Twos draw many people into their lives who teach them lessons about love. They benefit when working in partnerships and groups. These folks are not overly aggressive. They strive for peace and harmony.

Since Twos are here to work on affairs of the heart and getting along with others, close ties are important. Friendships, family, and other  loved ones will be major players in a Two's life. Many of these relationships have a fated quality about them; perhaps dealing with past-life issues and karma.

Some Twos find relationships troubling. Either they can't meet the "right one," or they have a problem with settling down, even though they desperately want to. This is all part of the lesson they are here to learn. Not only do Twos need other people, but they need to learn about the mechanics of relationships; what it takes to make love work, along with compromise and balance.

Romance is so important for Twos. Girls often fantasize about their wedding day years before it happens. Guys long to be the knight in shining armor for their princess. Both sexes believe in the theory of soul mates.

If Twos are dateless or single for long, they feel empty. It's really important for them to be in a steady relationship. In preteen years, they have posters of music and movie idols plastered all over their bedroom walls. In later teen years, their love life is sometimes more important than good grades in school. They can't go to the prom without a date—it's unthinkable! If dating, they are joined at the hip with the object of their affections.

Because Twos get so caught up in love, they can neglect their friends. This is an area they need to work on. If your friend is a Two and currently single, don't count on things staying the same in your relationship when she falls in love. She really doesn't mean to dismiss you, it's just love consumes her. (When there's a break-up—and there eventually will be—guess whose shoulder she'll come to cry on?) If you are a Two, it's important to keep a balance in your everyday life between all of your relationships—friends and lovers.

Love is grand, but don't miss out on all of the other wonderful things your teenage years have to offer!

Famous Number Twos: Gwen Stefani and Madonna

NUMBER THREE

Threes are communicators. They are creative and imaginative. Many make excellent teachers, writers, and artists. Some are quick-witted and have a good sense of humor. Their minds are constantly ticking.

Education and learning new things excite these teens. Most are open to try new things. However, some Threes can be too cautious and don't take enough chances. It's important that they don't allow fear or phobias to deny them experiences that will enrich their lives. Ride the roller coaster at least once!

Threes place a big emphasis on friendships. They enjoy going out in groups. The social scene is important and they love just hanging out. Travel is a big deal too. Bribe them with a set of wheels and they'll do anything!

Some Threes are known for their elaborate collections; from Beanie Babies to tea cups to race car models. Their collections usually are valuable and they keep them for years, hating to part with memorabilia mostly because of sentimental value.

Those born with this birth number can be a little fickle in love. They like variety and change, but once they make a commitment, it's usually solid. Threes want a boyfriend or girlfriend who will really listen to them. They want someone they can share their deepest feelings with. It's important to feel they are listened to and taken seriously in a relationship.

With a natural-born gift of gab, these teens can burn up the phone lines! They enjoy good gossip and are known to be blabbermouths! Don't tell a Three your darkest secret unless you want it broadcast all over third period!

Threes are good-hearted people though. They usually keep friends for life, all the way from kindergarten to old age. They'll remember your birthday every year!

If you're a Three, you should make sure to use all of your instinctive creative talents. We all are born with a special gift. It is our responsibility to the universe to use these gifts to help others in some way. Threes are blessed with a variety of talents: creativity, musical ability, communication skills, and teaching capabilities. So, if you have a beautiful voice, make music with it. If you can write, become a reporter or novelist. If you excel in a certain subject, teach others to excel too. By helping others, your talent will grow! If you don't use it, you'll lose it. Giving of yourself and helping others along their spiritual path is why we're all on planet Earth anyway!

Famous Number Threes: Selma Blair, Eminem, Drew Barrymore, and Cameron Diaz

NUMBER FOUR

If you're a Number Four, you are dependable and trustworthy. You are often more mature than your peers. Fours like to help others, but need to be appreciated for their efforts. Family ties are very important. You are likely to be close to your mother.

Fours are serious and studious and usually do well in school. Some Fours need an extra push to go out into the world. They want to succeed—and often do—but "Home Sweet Home" is hard to leave.

They are most happy once they have a spouse and children of their own. Yes, they can be homebodies, but if given the right kind of encouragement, Fours can be dynamite in the outside world.

These are "salt-of-the-earth" people. If you're a Four, people know they can depend on you. You will hate to be late for anything. You're also the friend who never forgets your best bud's birthday, your parent's anniversary, and to call your grandma. Family heirlooms, genealogy, and the family tree are things you hold dear. A sense of belonging to something is important, whether it be your school team, 4-H Club, or community youth council. Sharing with others and working together makes you feel happy and secure.

You're probably good with little kids. You may have a special connection with your pets. You can sense other people's pain and feel empathy for others. Because of these nurturing qualities, Fours make great doctors, nurses, counselors, and teachers.

Fours need to feel as if they fit in and "belong" and usually try hard to please people. They want everyone to like them, so they may go overboard to win approval. Some are perfectionists.

In relationships, Fours like to date one person at a time, and a relationship can last all the way through high school and college. Some marry their childhood sweethearts.

Fours' lesson is to take more risks and try new things. If you don't accept change, or hang on too tightly to the past, you could get stuck in ruts and life becomes boring.

Your life is what you make it, filled with challenges, opportunities, and new experiences. Think outside of the box once in a while and you'll be pleasantly surprised!

Famous Number Fours: Will Smith, Usher, Avril Lavigne, and Demi Moore

NUMBER FIVE

Fives are creative and love change. They are here to conquer the world and usually have a lot of goals they want to accomplish. Many are into music, art, and creative writing. Their minds are strong and many have high IQs. They just don't like to sit long enough to prove it! Sometimes Fives enjoy the chase more than the conquest. They enjoy striving for a goal rather than reaching it.

In love, Fives can date more than one person at a time and enjoy playing the field. Flirting is a favorite pastime and they master the art like no other! Fives don't always need to be in a relationship. They feel comfortable in their own company and are known to go without

 a steady relationship for years. These guys and girls are hard to tie down for long! Some have been known to be footloose and fancy-free well into their thirties.

Change is important to Fives. If their life is too steady or complacent, they'll stir the pot a little and cause a bit of ruckus just to keep the party going! And speaking of parties, Fives throw the best bashes. Because they are spontaneous, anything can happen. If you have a friend who is a Five, you will find him great fun to hang out with. There's never a dull moment.

These kids always seem to land on their feet. In sticky situations, they come out smelling like a rose. If they get caught skipping school or cheating on a test, their punishment doesn't always fit the crime. They get away with a lot.

Fives win popularity contests. Seldom do people talk badly about them, except for their jilted boyfriends and girlfriends! Lucky in love, they could break a few hearts along the way. Fives don't mean to hurt anyone, they just look at life as one big party.

Therefore, Fives can't decide what they really want to do when they grow up. There are too many choices. You may find them changing their college majors more than once. They'll work a lot of odd jobs, never staying too long in any one place. When they get older, however, they do settle down.

Fives are the type of people that make millions with their own inventions or happen to fall into something. They are at the right place at the right time. Experiences are what life is about. "Live life to its fullest," "You only go around once," and "Make the most of every day" are some of the mottos Fives live by!

Famous Number Fives: Kelly Osbourne, Sarah Michelle Gellar, Paul Walker, and Beyoncé Knowles

If you're a Number Six, you may prefer a structured and disciplined life. You are apt to be concise, intellectual, and a deep thinker. Most Sixes have their lives planned out at about age seven or so. They know what they want to do when they get older, or have a good idea of what they don't want to! Many find jobs while in their teen years, and are good, honest, dependable workers.

Sixes have their share of luck and then some. They can attain great wealth if they work hard at it. They do enjoy the finer things that life has to offer, along with the status symbols: expensive sports cars and designer clothes.

Most of these people are attractive and charis-matic. Often they are found taking on leadership roles. People look up to them. They run the risk of an inflated ego if they're not careful, but Sixes are mostly down-to-earth.

You will find many success stories among Sixes. In younger years, these kids were known to be teacher's pet, winning awards, and playing on the all-star team. In teenage years, Sixes will have their share of trophies too.

Sixes seem to be able to fit a great deal into their lives: school, work, an internship, a volunteer group, and helping their parents with younger siblings. Their lives are always full of things to do. Sixes grow up to be the supermoms and corporate fathers who squeeze anything and everything into an eighteen-hour day.

Success is usually theirs because Sixes work hard for it. Sixes have priorities. Most of the time doing well in school is at their top of the list, followed by work, and then a social life.

In relationships, Sixes are not mushy romantics. They are polite, reserved, and respectful. Appearances matter; they feel the person they date is a reflection of themselves. Often they will wish to date the best-looking guy or the most popular girl in the class. What others think of them matters, but not nearly as much as what they think of themselves.

Famous Number Sixes: Steven Spielberg, Ben Affleck, Anna Paquin, and Justin Timberlake

NUMBER SEVEN

The positive traits of Number Sevens are compassion and generosity. If you are a Seven, you were probably kind to all of your playmates as a child. If someone was hurt, you tried to comfort him.

Sevens are also very witty. They have a great sense of humor, and know exactly what to say to make everyone smile!

Sevens can be very romantic and a make delightful boyfriends or girlfriends. They have their share of dates and admirers. They are honest with their feelings, but do not like to fight or argue. Sometimes they will avoid confrontations, but when a love affair turns sour, they can walk away.

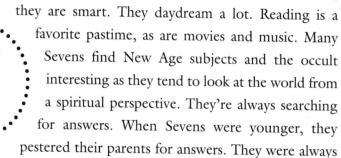

Although Sevens are not usually at the top of their class in school, they are smart. They daydream a lot. Reading is a favorite pastime, as are movies and music. Many Sevens find New Age subjects and the occult interesting as they tend to look at the world from a spiritual perspective. They're always searching for answers. When Sevens were younger, they pestered their parents for answers. They were always asking "Why?" They were curious about the mysteries of life. In teen years, Sevens are still searching, but have either developed faith in or skepticism about in the world around them.

Sevens are fascinating people. They are interesting to talk to. They have a lot of friends in and out of school and, surprisingly, of all ages. They have several best friends: one at school, one at church, one in the neighborhood . . . you get the picture?

Some Sevens are very psychic individuals. They're born with a sixth sense, and, if nurtured and developed, can use their intuitive powers to get ahead in life. They make good counselors, business people, ministers, politicians, lawyers, and negotiators. A positive attitude is one their greatest attributes. They believe in equality, fairness, and social justice. Therefore, so many are drawn to humanitarian causes, whether it be in their own school, community, or helping society as a whole. Sevens want to help make the world a better place in which to live. Many can and do make a difference.

> **Famous Number Sevens:** Ashton Kutcher, Seann William Scott, Mary-Kate and Ashley Olsen, and Natalie Portman

NUMBER EIGHT

Consider yourself lucky if you're an Eight. Eights draw money to them easily. You're one hard worker who'll get a raise without having to ask for it. Or you'll be showered with beautiful gifts and a great clothing allowance. College scholarships may drop at your feet. Grandpa has a trust fund set up for you. Eights are born into money and are often spoiled. If their family is not considered wealthy, parents work hard to give their child the extras only money can buy.

As Eights grow up, they want to make their own money and are determined to go after a good job that pays well. Many become affluent and quite successful. However, they should learn not to take everything so seriously and that money isn't everything. Often Eight children will work in the family business and forgo prom and football games because a job is more important to them. Take the time to  relax and enjoy life. The money will be there. Work will be there. There's plenty of time for all of that. Remember to enjoy your teenage and young adult years. They are something you can never return to once they've passed.

Eights are always coming up with ways to make another buck or convince dad they need an extra twenty. Some people call them hustlers. Others will say they're aggressive go-getters. They know one day they'll be rich!

If you're an Eight, status symbols and nice clothes are important. Designer labels are a must. Even though you're not always into the latest fads, "fitting in" is important. Keeping up with the Joneses is *very* important. It's not that Eights are all materialistic. They want money to enjoy life, to be able to afford experiences, like traveling to Europe in the summer, going to the latest movies, having a nice music system, and, of course, treating friends every now and then. Eights are generous people and enjoy giving as much as they do receiving.

When it comes to affairs of the heart, Eights can be just as generous. Buying cute cards and little presents for their sweetie gives them much delight. When they fall in love, they fall hard and fast. They'll do whatever it takes to make a relationship work. Their hearts are sometimes even bigger then their wallets!

Eights' lesson is to learn to enjoy the true luxuries of life: people, home, family, and love.

 Famous Number Eights: Josh Hartnett, Shakira, Matt Damon, and Missy Elliott

Number nine is the most powerful number of all because it contains the qualities of all of the other numbers. Nine stands for energy and most Nines are full of life and vitality. They don't plan and plot a lot, they just act! They are strong-willed people and do not bend easily. Nines are restless souls and quite impulsive. They have quick tempers, but most of the time they are cheerful and optimistic.

As little kids, Nines can be monsters, but lov-able ones. They seem to get their way all of the time. That's because they never give in. Nines are accused of being spoiled brats, but it's not their fault! In their defense, the adults in their life made them so! They allowed them to get away  with things. It's hard to say no to their angelic faces and sweet pouts!

Nines usually do well in school. But if academics aren't their strong point, you'll find them using their talents in other ways to shine. Most want to cut mom's apron strings and leave home sooner than their brothers and sisters. They want to backpack cross-country, move to another state, or conquer the world! It is important for Nines to complete their education and enroll into a university or college. But their lust to see the world could deter them. This is not a good thing. Sometimes they don't go back to school. Their lives take a lot of twists and turns. Other things become priorities.

If Nines marry young (before age twenty-five), the union may end in divorce court. They should wait until their late twenties or early thirties to settle down. A relationship has more staying power by then. Their wanderlust is tamed and the Nine is ready to make a per-manent commitment.

It is so important that between the ages of eighteen and twenty Nines stay on a specific course or have a disciplined agenda. Otherwise, they could set themselves up for failure and it may take years to get back on track.

Upon graduation, college or a business plan should come first. Most Nines can conquer the world if they set out to do so, but it needs to be done in an orderly fashion to avoid unnecessary crisis.

 Famous Number Nines: Mahatma Gandhi, Kate Beckinsale, and Kirsten Dunst

NUMBER ELEVEN

If your birth number reduces down to eleven, then you need not reduce it down to two. Eleven is a special number in a special category outside the basic numerology system that covers numbers one to nine. Eleven is a master number. These people are considered higher spiritual beings. If you fall into this category, you have great psychic powers.

You can rise to the top in your chosen profession. There is no gray area for the Number Eleven. You are either very positive or very negative when it comes to your way of thinking.

 The positive Elevens achieve great things. The negative ones drift through life and appear cool and aloof. If you're an Eleven, you are blessed with special powers. Use them for your highest good. Don't waste the potential you have within you to accomplish great things!

You can dream big and those wishes can come true. The power of your mind is very strong. If you believe something will happen, it does. Say you want to own your business one day. You can easily imagine how your office is laid out. You visualize every little detail. You know in your heart you will be successful—there is no doubt! Things manifest for you. They just happen if you believe. It's almost effortless!

Love is the same way. Once you set your sights on that special someone, you have eyes for no one else. You can draw that person to you. Elevens can mesmerize people.

So, you have these wonderful spiritual gifts: intuitive powers, the ability to manifest great things, and powerful attraction. What do you do with them? These are presents from the universe. Open them, use them correctly and for your highest good. If you work from your heart out of an unselfish and giving attitude, the entire world opens up to you. Seize your inner power, channel it correctly, and make all of your dreams come true!

Famous Number Elevens: Prince William, Lucy Liu, Mark Wahlberg, and Orlando Bloom

NUMBER TWENTY-TWO

These are unique and special individuals. Number Twenty-two is the number of the truly exceptional person. If the qualities of the Twenty-two are developed, they combine all of the best influences from the other numbers and one can achieve greatness. Twenty-two possesses the following strength or character from each of the other ten numbers:

#1: Intelligence

#2: Sensitivity

#3: Energy

#4: Ethics and diligence

#5: Ambition

#6: Charisma

#7: Psychic vision

#8: Determination

#9: Courage

#11: Idealism

If not developed, Twenty-twos can be dreamers and schemers. Some are workaholics and can be arrogant. But if the Twenty-two people use the abilities they have, they can go very far in life. The true purpose in their life should be service to others. Because they have such a vast array of great abilities, they should share their talents and resources with others. Do you know someone special? Do you say to yourself, "That guy has it all: charisma, luck, success"? He could be a Number Twenty-two who is using the magic of his birth number correctly.

If you're a Twenty-two, please recognize that you have great power within you. You have been placed on this planet to do extraordinary things with this power. Yes, you could be the president some day. You could help develop a world peace plan. You may be an Oscar-winning actor in a few years. You could be famous. *You* can make a difference in the world. Don't ever give up on a wish or a desire. If it is for your highest good, it will happen. You just need to  learn more patience. This is the lifetime in which you can reach goals most people would consider out of reach. Don't let negative people say you can't accomplish a goal. If you believe it, you can achieve it. You are blessed. Please don't waste this lifetime. It would be crime to do so!

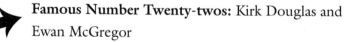 **Famous Number Twenty-twos:** Kirk Douglas and Ewan McGregor

You've discovered your birth number and the personality traits associated with it. Now let's look at predictive numerology. I've designed my own numerology formula to help you predict the next nine years of your life. This is a simple formula that's easy to learn. You'll amaze your family and friends when you do a reading for them. I've used this method for thousands of clients over the past ten years and it has never failed.

In this numerology formula, our lives run in nine-year cycles. Each cycle has a different meaning. We deal with different issues and emphasis is placed on a certain path in our life each year. The cycles run birthday to birthday rather than calendar year to calendar year. This is important to remember. I will explain the different cycles shortly.

It is extremely important to remember this numerology does not run calendar year to calendar year. It runs from your birthday to your next birthday. For example, if your next birthday falls on December 31, 2003, you cannot use the master number for 2003 until you reach your birthday. You will still be working off 2002's master number until the end of 2003. If your next birthday is April 1, 2004, you will be working off the 2003 master number for the first four months of the calendar year. Then, in April, begin using the 2004 master number.

PREDICTIVE NUMEROLOGY FORMULA

For now, here's the formula you'll need to discover your numerology number for the year. First step: take your birth month and add it to your day of birth (do *not* include the year). Example:

$$\text{June } 4 = 6 + 4 = 10$$

This is the tricky part: you add the above number to the current year's master number:

2002—40
2003—41
2004—42   10
2005—43   + 41 (current year's master number)
2006—44   ―――
2007—45   51
2008—46
2009—47
2010—48
2011—49

Take that last number and reduce it down to its lowest single digit.

$$51 = 5 + 1 = 6$$

There you have your number for the year. In the example, it's the number six.

This is a year of bright, beautiful beginnings. The emphasis is on *you*! Your needs, wishes, and dreams will be the focus. I always tell my clients when you are in your Number One year, you can get *anything* you want, but you need to ask for it. No one is going to hand you anything on a silver platter. You may have to ask more than once for your heart's desire, but it's likely that you will receive it.

Anyone coming into a Number One year should take the time to make up a wish list. This is most effective when done on your birthday. The list should include everything you want, big and small. It doesn't matter if some of the things sound silly. Just write them down. This is *your* year. Your list can include more money, a new love, good grades, a scholarship, a dream car, or a new best friend. I recall a friend of my mine who put "a new boyfriend" at the top of her list on her June birthday. By October, she was going steady with a great guy! I made up my wish list and got thirteen out of the fourteen wishes over the course of the twelve months.

The thing to remember when you make your list is to be very specific. You could say, "I want guys to notice me," and you'll probably get asked out by every jerk in town! But if you were to write, "I want to meet a nice, cute guy this summer," chances are he'll be to your liking! Write "I want a job I will enjoy that pays ten dollars an hour," rather than "I want a new job." The more details, the better!

Number One years are good for landing a new job where you'll take on more responsibility and learn new skills. The new friends that enter your life now will be beneficial to you in some way. If you're starting a new school or moving, expect things to go well. Number

One years are for any type of new beginning and they can influence how the next nine years of your life pans out. So make the most of this time.

NUMBER TWO YEAR

Are you looking for love? This year is a good time to find it! Your Number Two year is a period in which new relationships come into your life, romance blossoms, and you are ready to fall madly in love! If all of your friends are dating, you will want to find a special someone too. If you're single this year, you may get a little depressed if you don't have a date every Friday night. Therefore, you should be

more aggressive in love. This is the year to take the chance and ask someone out. You'll be pleasantly surprised. If your friends want to fix you up on a blind date, it may not be a bad idea. Go ahead and go! Love could be right around the corner.

If you are in a steady relationship already, this could be a deeper commitment year. Problems? You two can work through them easily now.

Even your friendships flow smoother this year. Love seems to be flowing through everyone you meet. This is a year many teens discover their first love!

By the time the Number Two year is in full swing, most people are happy with their love life. If you're not, it may be time to think about breaking new ground. Get out and travel in new circles, meet new people, make new friends. This year, anything can happen in love. Be sure to always look your best when you go out, because you'll never know who you'll meet. A real hottie could be eyeing you at the mall or the local library.

One of the dangers of the Number Two year is that you could be so infatuated with someone, all you want to do is be with that person. You daydream all the time when you're apart and it's hard to concentrate on anything else. Remember to keep on top of your studies so you don't fall behind in your classes. Don't get caught making goggle eyes or blowing kisses in the school hallways!

NUMBER THREE YEAR

Communication, travel, and creative pursuits fill this cycle. You won't feel much like hitting the books. Your popularity is on the rise and you'll be attending lots of parties and special events.

New and long-lasting friendships could develop. Any clubs or organizations you join will benefit you greatly. Let the good times roll! This is a year to hang out with the crowd and enjoy life. Have all the fun you can handle now, because when your Number Four year rolls around, there won't be time.

Your social life is in full swing and frankly, that's all you'll care about this year. There's plenty of party invitations. Your day planner will be filled. It will be hard to find you home much now. You're on the run all the time. This year you could get a new car or sign up for driver's education courses too.

Your personal spending habits may get out of control as you find yourself at the mall more. Music, CD players, your own television set, and a personal computer are "must-haves." You could get your own phone line. Dad may buy you a cell phone. Set limits; don't let the talk time get out of hand. Your bills will be higher than you ever imagined!

Friends will make huge demands on your time. You may have to prioritize to get homework done on schedule. Study groups may help. You'll be tempted to cut class now and then; not a good idea, as you could fall behind in your studies due to increased social activities.

New best friends will enter your life, and with them, exciting, fun things to do every weekend. If you're invited to join a youth group or sit on student council, your presence will be a good thing. Any type of group involvement, whether it be social or academically inclined, is favorable.

This is also a year that your family takes a great vacation! Don't stay home and feed the cats, go along. You'll be glad you did. You will love to travel this year and can't get enough of the great outdoors. Sports and hobbies will expand. Your personal interests shine too. This is your "fun" year. Enjoy it, but keep a balance in your life at the same time.

NUMBER FOUR YEAR

This is the best year to make the honor roll at school or get a job. You can increase your income too. If you do, it will be through your own hard work.

Your social life takes a back seat. Often your love life will be dull, or you'll be too busy working to notice. You won't have as much time to spend with friends. Most teens get a new job and work hard trying to balance sports, homework, and weekend chores. You'll be thinking about serious issues this year, such as your future and college choices.

Much can be gained if you work hard. You'll feel good about the paths that are opening up for you, and be more serious about your goals. Using your time wisely is a must. This is a year in which you will feel successful, as if your hard work is paying off. If you've been studying hard, your grades will improve. If you are attending basketball practice religiously, it will show on the court. There will be more recognition and reward for your time and effort.

Opportunities may drop in your lap. You could be offered summer jobs. Your parents, teachers, and boss will praise you more than ever. There will be times when you'll have to choose between work and play, between hanging out with your friends or clocking in on a Saturday night. Work will likely win out.

In fact, it will seem as if all you do is work. You'll beat a path from school to practice to study hall to work and then back again. Know that your hard work is not in vain. You are gaining ground. You are getting ahead. Things will slow down a little and there will be more time to relax when your Number Five year rolls around. For now, you will make more money than ever before.

Promotions are likely. Ask for a raise at work—you'll get it. The interesting thing about a Number Four year is you really want to work. You look forward to it. If there's a job you've had your eye on, this is the year to put in an application. Many teens land their first job and gain valuable contacts and experience during their Number Four cycle.

NUMBER FIVE YEAR

This is the year to fall madly in love! This is also a time when you'll have many romantic options. It seems as if everyone is interested in you. You may have your eye on more than one person too! Know that you will attract some wonderful people, but you'll draw your share of losers as well!

A Number Five year can coincide with your "first love." The guy or girl you meet this year will be one you won't ever forget. You may easily hang on to the memory of this special person for years. Because it is also a romantic time, you could easily get lost in a fantasy world or caught up in daydreams. This is not a major commitment year, but the mate you meet now could lead to a deeper promise or engagement if you're still together two years from now.

You will love all of the attention and want to date as much as you can. Hormones are raging too, and if you are sexually active, you run the risk of a pregnancy this year. Take precautionary measures or abstain altogether if you want to avoid this aspect. This is a time when you could feel pressured by your peers about sex. Talk with your parents, teachers, or counselors if you feel confused about your feelings.

A lot of teens move or enroll in a new school during a Number Five year. Just as many find their families remodeling the house or buying a vacation home somewhere. Five is a year of change and it's mostly good. If you want to redecorate your room, your folks will probably agree that it's time to get rid of the kiddy wallpaper and replace it with a more updated look.

You'll want to update your personal look too. Changes in hairstyles, new clothes, and a new attitude emerge now. You're defining who you are by the way you look and dress. Braces come off, ears get pierced, and acne clears up.

There will be many changes this year regarding your likes and dislikes too. If you always loved cookies and cream, now you are ordering rocky road. Your tastes in fashion and friends is changing too. It's a bittersweet year—letting the past go, crossing the bridge from a little kid to young adult—but change is good!

The Number Six cycle is a year in which you have a strong desire to get your life in order. If you're not happy with your grades, you'll work to improve them. If you hate your baby-sitting job, you'll send out résumés. If your circle of friends becomes boring, you'll look elsewhere for fun.

This is a good time to break bad habits. You can stop biting your nails now. You'll hand your homework in on time. *Organization* is this year's buzzword. The Six year is when you get rid of what's not working for you and replace it with something that will. You'll toss out old toys collecting dust in your attic. You'll pitch third-grade spelling papers and out-of-date fashions too. You hate clutter. Mom will be happy because your room will be clean!

Other people will put restrictions on you now. Parents will enforce strict rules and curfews. Teachers won't budge an inch on test scores and sliding-scale grades. You'll have to work hard and color in the lines this year!

However, if there is something you wish to accomplish, you can do it now. This is a great time to lose weight if you need to, get in shape, or undergo intense physical training. If you set your mind to do something, determination and willpower will see you through. The power of your mind is very strong and there is little that you can't succeed at.

Some people say the Number Six year is boring. Nothing exciting happens. That is somewhat true. Six is not about excitement and fun. It's about organization, duty, and responsibility. You will feel more grown up and responsible this year. The universe is calling on you to mature and make good solid decisions.

So, if you're waiting to get your life in order or to clean up your act, the Number Six year calls on you to do this. It will help you accomplish much if you truly want to.

NUMBER SEVEN YEAR

This is what I call your "legal" year. If of age, this year you'll get your driver's license, work permit, and maybe even cosign for a loan. Anything your name is on looks good. So, put out those resumes for a new job, ask for a raise by putting your request in writing. You may even see your picture in the newspaper now. You see, the Seven year is a time for more recognition. You will stand out in a crowd. People notice you now and acknowledge your accomplishments. Go ahead— toot your own horn!

Your grades should be improving this year, and opportunities that arise can be most advantageous. You may make the honor roll at school, or be employee of the month at work. If you are on the debate team, giving speeches, or in the school play, your star will shine brightly. Auditions for modeling, drama club, and cheerleading

go well. Apply for college scholarships now if possible.

You could also be lucky. Entering drawings and raffles is a good idea. If you are job hunting, it's important that you write a personal letter with your resume. Superiors will appreciate your extra effort. Some older teens may sign with the army or navy at this time.

The number seven is also a very spiritual number, so this year will be filled with higher thinking on your part. You could become enlightened about a spiritual path or have a strong desire to study occult matters. Many people connect with their spirit guides or guardian angel this year. You may have a strong desire to study different religions. People you meet will likely have a profound effect on your life at this time. New mentors could appear. You will be feeling more intuitive during this period and will likely expand your own psychic abilities.

If you're applying for scholarships, running for student council, or trying out for a sports team, you'll likely be successful.

Anything you're involved in legally should go well. If you have to fight a traffic fine in court, you will do well. If an officer pulls you over for speeding, you can talk your way out of a ticket. However, mom and dad may not be quite as understanding.

NUMBER EIGHT YEAR

You could hit the jackpot this year! This is an excellent money period. The Eight year brings money to you effortlessly. Financial rewards do not always have to come via parents or part-time jobs. Expensive gifts, clothes, and trips could come your way. Since you will have more money at your disposal, you can invest in hobbies and other interests.

This is a great time to ask for a raise in your allowance or at your job. Everywhere you go, you'll run into good deals, sales, and money opportunities. A lot of kids find they start a serious savings plan. Whether you stash some cash in your dresser drawer or open an account at your local bank, your money will grow.

Shop around now for the best deals because you will certainly find some. Parents and relatives are ready to help you out if you need extra spending money. Instead of receiving lots of birthday gifts this year, people are more likely to give you cash. You can accumulate a lot if you plan wisely. Just don't think this trend is going to last forever. Put some money away for a rainy day. You'll be glad you did.

The Number Eight year is also a fine time to be thinking about new ways to make money. If you have business skills and would like to operate your own part-time service-oriented company, now is the time to go after some funding and get started. You'll be surprised how much you make with little effort. If you baby-sit on weekends, you may raise your hourly rate or charge extra for holidays and special occasions. Don't take anything for granted or dismiss opportunities now. Opportunities could come out of the blue to bring you extra money.

Sometimes the Eight cycle is not consistent. You could have lots of extra spending money one week, then feel broke the next, but if you really need cash for something, it will be there.

Many teenagers receive inheritances during this period, scholarship funding, and their first credit card applications arrive in the mail! Don't be afraid to speak up now for a raise or more money. Let people know your skills, time, and energy are worth something.

NUMBER NINE YEAR

This year wraps up your entire nine-year cycle. Here, we deal with the karma of the past eight years—in other words, lessons you still need to learn or debts you need to repay.

Anything you didn't do or handle correctly in the previous cycles you must address now. You have no choice.

Some people fear the approaching Nine year. Others are not  affected by it at all because they have lived their cycles correctly.

Many times the past will come back to haunt you. For instance, if you ended a relationship badly with your ex, you'll probably meet up to make amends. Likewise if you have been waiting for your old boyfriend to kiss and make up, this is the year he waltzes back into your life. This is also a time some of you could be graduating, ending friendships, moving, or quitting a dead-end job.

Your Number Nine year doesn't always bring bad luck, but most of us don't follow the straight and narrow. There are usually some things we must contend with. The least you will experience is a feeling of being "held back." It's as if you can't get ahead, no matter how hard you push. The universe is telling you to slow down. Allow yourself time to reflect. You'll be up and running when the Number One year hits on your next birthday.

CHAPTER 3

IN THE PALM OF YOUR HAND

YOUR FUTURE AND PALMISTRY

Your palms have a story to tell—a story about you, your life, and where it is headed. Did you ever imagine you'd find your future in the palm of your hand?

The art of palmistry has been studied and used for centuries to predict health, financial success, and love. These days, anyone who can read a book can learn to read their own palms. To read yours, here's what you need:

A magnifying glass

Pen and paper

Two clean hands

When studying the palms, you should read both, but most people read their dominant hand. If you're right-handed, read your right hand. If you're a lefty, use the left hand. The opposite palm can tell what your karma is. Sometimes it represents your potential. The dominant hand represents your future and can tell you all sorts of wonderful things, like your character, personality, how many times you'll be married, how many kids you'll have, and much more.

Did you know that the lines in your palm change? Just because you read your palm once doesn't mean it stays the same. As you grow and experience new things, the lines will change. The lines reflect some of your new attitudes and talents you've developed. Lines can grow longer, shorten, and even disappear altogether! If you were to read your palm every six months or so, you would be surprised at how many lines change. There are also some lines that don't appear until you grow older.

There are major lines in your palms such as the life line and the heart line. And there are many minor lines such as the fate line. The minor ones develop as you get older and experience life. Most kids under age ten don't have a fate line. Then when people grow old, they lose some of their lines or they become shorter. When elderly people suffer memory loss, the lines in their palms seem to fade or blur.

Let's find out more about you. What can your palm tell you about the future?

The diagram on the next page will show you the major lines in your palm. They are:

The life line

The heart line

The head line

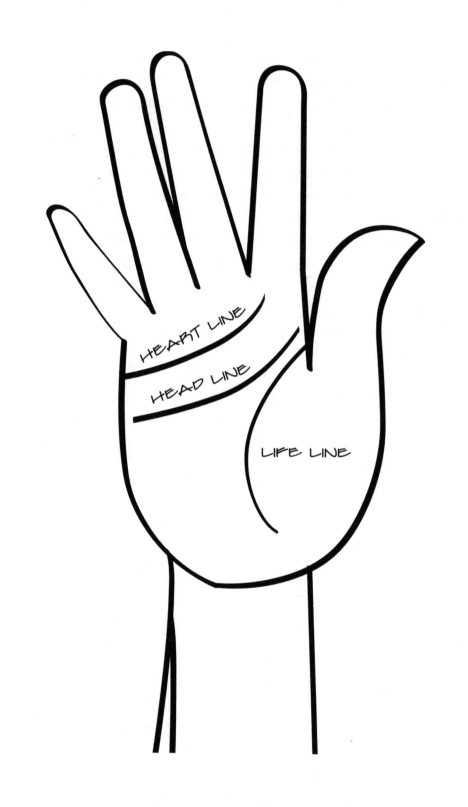

If you can find these three lines, you can learn the basics of palm reading. These three major lines can help you understand a lot about your personality. Remember to read both palms. Your dominant hand will show you the person you have become because of your upbringing and life circumstance. Your other hand shows what potential you were blessed with and maybe even your karma! Further study could provide you a sneak peak into your past lives and the lessons you brought over into this one!

EXAMINING YOUR LINES

Key questions to ask yourself:

1. Are your lines deep or shallow?

2. Are your lines wide or narrow?

3. Are there breaks, forks, or other indentations in your lines?

4. Are your lines curved or straight?

5. Where do the lines begin and end?

Draw your lines on the palms provided on the next page or another piece of paper if you wish.

Notes: The head and the life lines are read from the inside of the palm near the thumb to the outside of the palm. The heart line is read the opposite way—from the outside little finger to the inside.

DRAW THE LINES OF
YOUR PALM HERE!

The lines will also show you an approximate time in your life for things to happen. You can "age" your lines very simply. Divide each line into seven even sections. Each section represents about ten years of your life. Most people will probably live longer, but we use ten-year increments. This will not give you an exact year or date, but will likely show more of a period—for example, childhood, young adult, old age, and so on.

See the diagram below to age a line.

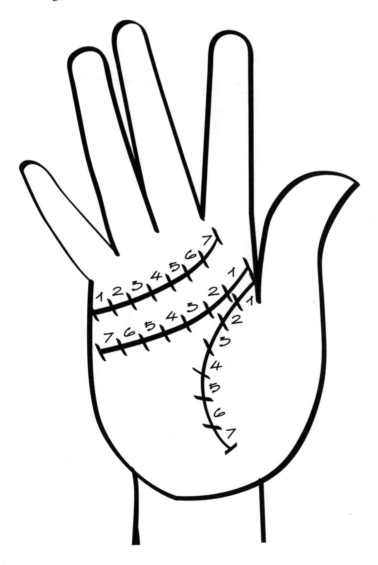

DRAW THE LINES
OF YOUR PALM HERE
AND AGE THEM!

PALM MARKING DEFINITIONS

Let's take a closer look at all of the little palm markings in your hand. They all can be easily interpreted. You may have a few of these in your palm. Read on for more details. A diagram on the next page shows an example of each.

Branch: A line branching off from the original line. It usually means a change or new direction: starting a new school, moving, a new job, and so on.

Cross: Two lines that are intersecting on a line means a struggle or hard times. The event or problem will be one you will not likely forget.

Star: Stars mean your dreams will come true. Stars mostly show up on the head or heart lines.

Triangle: Triangles are a good sign. These tell of happy times ahead.

Break: Breaks mean endings. If there is a break in your heart line, it could mean the end of a relationship. If the broken line begins in a new direction, it means a complete change and a new love interest.

Netting or meshing: This means stress and usually shows up in your palms when you're tired and overwhelmed by life.

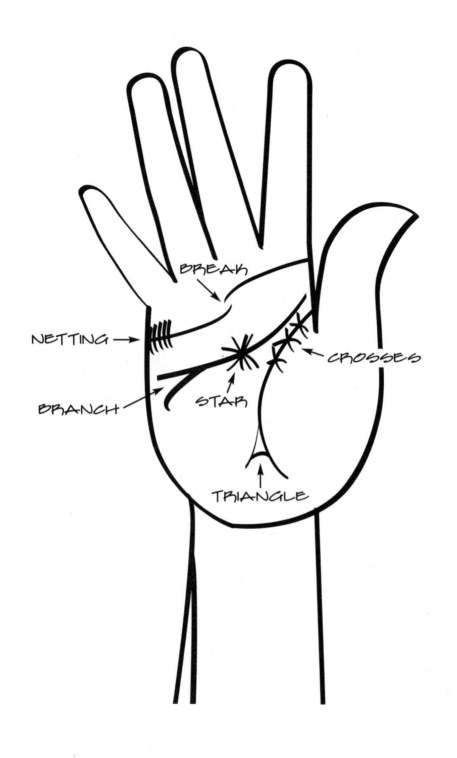

YOUR HEART LINE

Your heart line (also known as your love line) is the very top line in your palm. It starts a bit below your little finger and runs across the palm. The heart line will reveal information about your love life and how you deal with emotions. It will predict the ups and downs of your relationships over the next seventy years or so.

Draw your heart line on the next page. Remember to fill in all of the palm markings: the breaks, branches, and so on.

L'amour

LIEBE   *amor*

amore

LOVE

DRAW YOUR HEART
LINES HERE!

Now, let's interpret your heart line:

- Small branches that swing upward from the heart line mean you will have a happy love life and lots of good friends. The more upward branches you have, the more popular you will be.

- Branches in a downward direction mean heartbreak or disappointment in love and friendships.

- If your heart line curves up, you fall in love fast. You wear your heart on your sleeve and can get hurt easily. But you'll rebound quickly and be off to capture more hearts! Romance is very important to you. You are a passionate person. The bigger the curve, the more romantic you are!

- If the heart line is straight or has a small curve, you are cautious and not as apt to fall head over heels in love. You are loyal and will make a great husband or wife. You're a little too logical at times, and will need to make an extra effort to give hugs and kisses.

- Long, straight heart lines mean you are very intense, jealous, and possessive. You give 110 percent in a relationship, but can be a little controlling.

- If your heart line turns down at the end, it mean you can be moody and hard to deal with. You won't find this example much. Most heart lines curve upward. But if you're dating someone whose heart line turns down, you can expect the relationship to be stormy! If you have such a line, you may want to change some of your attitudes about love and be more optimistic.

Write down some things you have discovered about your heart line on the next page.

YOUR HEAD LINE

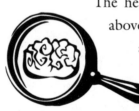

The head line is directly below the heart line and above the life line. Your head line will tell you about your talents, ambitions, how smart you are, and your abilities.

The head line is read from the pointer finger (sometimes called the index finger) next to your thumb across your palm.

Draw your head line on the next page. Remember to put in all of the palm markings.

DRAW YOUR HEAD
LINES HERE!

You're ready to interpret your head line:

- If your head line is cut deep and you can see it clearly, you are very intelligent. Deep lines also show confidence. A shallow line means you are intuitive but less confident. You could question yourself a lot. You are sentimental.

- If there's meshing or netting on this line, you need to learn to relax. You push yourself too hard. By aging this line, you can determine an approximate time to avoid stress.

- If your head line is straight, you're apt to be logical. Your mind will be strong throughout your entire life. Your memory will be good. You have strong willpower.

- A curved head line means you're creative. You can be enthusiastic but sometimes act before you think. You possess strong writing and acting skills.

- If your head line has a deep dip in it, you could be too sensitive. You also have to learn to follow though on things that you start. You can get all excited about a project, quickly lose interest, and drop it.

- If your head line ends in a fork, you can see both sides of a coin. If there is not a fork, you believe your way is the only way to do things!

- A lot of forks running throughout the head line represent many changes in your life.

- Large branches at the end of the line mean you have two different personalities. You could be serious yet fun-loving, saucy but sweet, and naughty but nice!

- If the head line ends in a fork with three branches, you are psychic. Not too many people have this configuration, but it's commonly seen in the palms of psychics and mediums.

- Branches in the head line mean events in your life. Downward branches mean troubling times. Branches going upward show happy events and successful periods.

- If your head line merges with your life line, your family and society will have a great influence on your life. If it doesn't, you will be independent and a bit of a rebel.

- The wider the space between the head and the life lines, the more independent you are.

- If a head and life line merge together and mesh appears at the beginning of these lines, you've experienced childhood traumas or crisis. If the meshing continues down the lines, it means you are still affected by things that happened to you in younger years.

- The longer your head line, the longer it takes you to make a decision. A shorter head line means you will make up your mind quicker and will not be as indecisive. However, there is a tendency to be impulsive.

Write down some things about your head line below.

THE LIFE LINE

The life line is the last major line. It starts in the inside of your palm above your thumb and runs to the base of your palm.

People always assume the life line predicts how long you will live. Not so! It really has to do with your physical well-being. If you have a short life line, don't freak out. It doesn't mean you'll die young. Remember your life line grows and changes as you do.

The life line will tell you about your health, your energy levels, and lifestyle changes.

Draw your life line on the next page. Remember to put in all of the palm markings.

DRAW YOUR LIFE
LINES HERE!

Now let's interpret your life line:

- Very deep lines mean you have lots of energy. You don't need as much rest as some of your friends, and are probably impatient with slow people. You are a bundle of energy.

- A shallow life line means you have low physical energy. You are apt to get tired quickly. If you have a shallow line here, make sure to get at least eight hours of sleep a night. Take your vitamins too, as you could be more prone to catching colds.

- Breaks in your life line can indicate illnesses or accidents. If your line breaks up and starts in another direction, it means you will overcome that difficulty.

- If there is a sudden break in your life line and then it starts up somewhere else, there will be a dramatic change in your life, per-haps even a lifestyle change.

- Branches and breaks in your life line can give you insight into things to come, but they can change. You can change things. We all have power of free will. So if you know there could be major break in your future, plan for it and be prepared!

- If you have branches shooting upward, this means you will achieve your goals. Downward branches mean disappointments in your ambitions. Breaks in the life line have more to do with physical problems, while branches have to do with emotional issues.

- A fork in your life line shows a decision needs to be made and it will be a major one.

- Chains on your life line can mean physical problems or minor health concerns. If you have a lot of chains, you could have allergies.

- If you have a curve that forms a half-circle from the inside of the thumb to the base of the palm, you like things peaceful. You're easy-going.

- If your life line swings wide, you love to travel. If it runs completely across your palm, you won't have an ordinary life. You will need change and new adventures to be happy. A wide life line without much of a curve means you are happy with just the basics and simple pleasures that life has to offer.

- If the life line clings to the thumb, you are a cautious person. You probably won't move far from home. Family and old friends are very important.

- If your life line curves widely around the thumb, you want to try everything once! You love nice things.

Write down some things you have learned about your life line below.

THE MINOR LINES

Minor lines do not appear on everyone's hands. You may not find any on your palms. Some of the lines do not develop until you get older. Others may never develop at all because they do not represent part of your personality. These lines include marriage, children, fate, and fame lines. Keep checking every few months though—one of these lines could turn up and you'll want to know exactly what it means!

THE FATE LINE

Of all the minor lines, I feel the fate line is the most important. It is also known as the karma or destiny line. It runs from the bottom of your hand up vertically through the middle of the palm. It will show you what you are supposed to do with your life—its true purpose and path.

It is important to read both fate lines in both palms. Your dominant hand will show how your fate line has changed because of the events in your life. The nondominant hand will show what your destiny was when you were born.

Draw your fate lines on the next page.

DRAW YOUR FATE
LINES HERE!

Let's examine your fate lines more closely:

- If the fate line in your dominant hand is well defined, you are an independent person. If you have a prominent fate line in your other hand but not in the dominant one, it means you have not used or reached your potential in life.

- The fate line can also tell you what career or job path you may excel in one day. If the fate line runs up the middle of your palm to your index (pointer) finger, you will be very ambitious in your career. You'd make a good business person, lawyer, or police officer.

- If the fate line moves straight up to the middle finger, you are a born leader. You would be good in politics, owning your own business, and supervising, managing, or teaching others.

- A fate line that lines up under one of your ring fingers shows you are a dramatic and creative person. You'd make a great actor, musician, or artist.

- If your fate line leans toward your little finger, journalism, writing, broadcasting, and teaching would be a career to consider.

- If your fate line starts in the middle of your palm, expect to become successful a little later in life. You may take a decade or so to decide what it is you want to do.

- If the fate line starts at the bottom of the palm and ends midway up, you'll start working at a young age and retire early.

- If your fate line doesn't start until it reaches the heart line, your love life will always be more important than work. Your world will center around those you love.

- If the fate line is deep, this means you are determined to succeed. Nothing will stand in the way of your goals.

- If there are a lot of breaks, there may be difficulties and career losses. Breaks also mean many different types of employment. You could bounce from one job to another.

- A line that is long and runs from the very bottom of the hand to the base of the fingers is the sign of the workaholic.

- A fate line that ends in a fork means a big decision or career change at some point in your life.

- A star at the bottom of the fate line means you will find success and happiness in your chosen career.

- For those who have no fate line, it merely means no set path has been made. You will create your own.

Write down what you have learned about your fate lines below.

THE FAME LINE

Do you have star quality? Will you be famous one day? Will your name be in lights? Not surprisingly, the fame line is not found in everyone's hand. But if you have one, it runs from the middle of your hand to the ring finger. Your fame line is on the outside of your fate line. It is usually fainter and harder to read. I suggest using your magnifying glass to see it more clearly.

Do you have a fame line? Draw it on the next page.

DRAW YOUR FAME
LINES HERE!

Let's interpret your fame line:

- A long fame line suggests that everyone adores you.

- If the fame line starts on your life line, you have star quality. Yes, you could be a famous entertainer one day!

- A fame line that branches off from your fate line means you will be famous because of your career.

- When the fame line starts from your head line, you could receive recognition because of a book you write or an invention you make. You will become famous because of your hard work.

- If the fame line starts at the heart line, you could marry someone who is famous, like a rock star or a Hollywood actor. The people you date or associate with could be well-known.

Write anything that you've learned about your fame line below.

Guys

Carson	~~~~	Braeden S.	Jerrod Shin
Caleb	Brendan V.	Josh T	Jeremy P.
Conrad	Brendan K.	Josh D	Nikit
hayden	Brandon h.	~~~~	Marko.
Kevin	Kris	Gary	Iman
Marc	Tristan N.	~~~~	~~~~
Simon	Tristan C.	Jeff Chao S.	
Sidoni	Brad.	Jonathon Li	

Alex Sosha   Stephen Tsui
Alex B.   Taylor Janzen.
Robert
Alex Kazemi?   Tyler W.
Gabe

Guest List.

Girls

Dawn   Niki   Erika
Amanda W.   Jessica?   Shaheena
Jenna   Kirstin
Britney   Vikki.
Sam   Kristen
Nicole   Alyssa   Rachel
Lindsey   Courts   Rania
Jocelyn   Crystal   Becca
Brianna   Danielle   Winnie
Maggi   Terry   Jessica
Aysha
Natasha   Wendy   Alethea   Sara
Austin   Alexis

33

MARRIAGE LINES AND CHILDREN LINES

Marriage lines are short horizontal lines under your little finger, almost to the edge of the palm. The lines that go up and down and through the marriage lines are called your children lines. They represent how many kids you're likely to have. You will need a magnifying glass to read these. The marriage lines can tell how many trips down the aisle you'll make and other interesting things about committed relationships.

Draw your marriage lines on the next page.

DRAW YOUR MARRIAGE
LINES HERE!

Let's interpret the marriage lines:

- Short, feathered lines mean short relationships that go nowhere. Longer, deeper lines mean more steady relationships are in your future.

- A single deep line stands for long-term commitment or one marriage.

- Two deep lines equal two long-term marriages.

- If you have several lines, you can expect a lot of relationships and commitments. Usually the number of lines represent the number of marriages.

- If the marriage line ends in a fork, that marriage will end in divorce.

Write what you've learned about your marriage lines below.

DRAW YOUR CHILDREN LINES HERE!

Children lines go up and down though the marriage lines. Because you are young, these lines may be very faint or not show up at all—just yet.

If you have found there are lines here, count the lines. This is likely the number of kids you will have.

Write below what you've learned about your children lines.

There are many more minor lines in your palms with fascinating stories to tell and secrets to reveal. Palmistry is like your own personal road map. But remember, you still drive the car! Your life's direction is ultimately up to you.

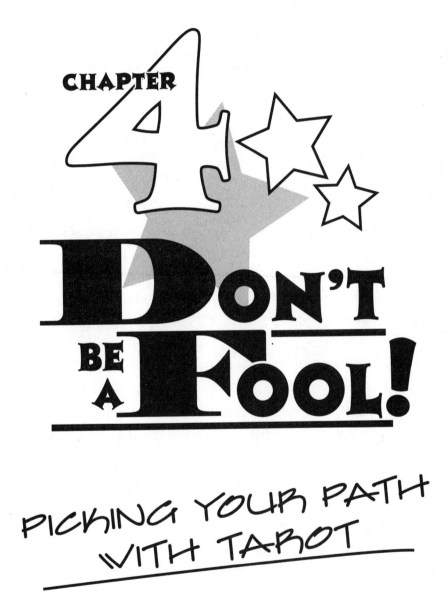

CHAPTER 4

DON'T BE A FOOL!

PICKING YOUR PATH WITH TAROT

The ancient art of tarot reading has been used for centuries all over the world. In the past century, tarot reading has been looked upon as more of a New Age form of divination, but there's nothing "new" about it. The tarot can be traced back to the eleventh century in the Far East. These cards were modeled more after a regular deck of playing cards than the tarot sets we see today. Gypsies used the tarot for years and are said to have brought the cards into Europe where they enjoyed great popularity. In the Middle Ages, hundreds of different types of tarot card sets were designed.

Even though the tarot underwent many facelifts and artistic changes, its messages remained the same, even to this day. There is a massive amount of ancient spiritual wisdom alive in the cards. The tarot combines belief systems such as the Hebrew Cabala, astrology, and numerology. Today you can walk into any New Age bookstore and find dozens of different tarot designs. There are Goddess cards, a Native American tarot, animal tarot, Halloween tarot, and even baseball card sets. They may all have different pictures, but the meanings in the cards remain the same.

The tarot is nothing to be scared of, but it is to be respected. Taken seriously and considered a sacred tool, it can help you unlock some of the mysteries of life and what lies before you. There are seventy-eight cards in the tarot deck. There are twenty-two major arcana cards and fifty-six minor arcana. *Arcana* means "profound secrets."

In this chapter you will learn what each of the cards mean, and how to give three different basic readings.

WHAT KIND OF CARDS SHOULD YOU GET?

If you're serious about learning and reading tarot, then you will want to get a good, high-quality deck of cards. As I mentioned, there are possibly thousands of different types of tarot cards on the market today. How do you choose one? I suggest you go to a bookstore or a New Age store that offers a good selection. Then pick through the cards that you are drawn to the most. What appeals to you? If there are sample decks that are already open, look through them. Ask if you can open a deck you are particularly interested in. Feel how the deck fits in your hand. Fan the cards out. What feelings do you get from them? Do you feel good about the cards? Shuffle them. Do you still feel drawn to them? If the answer is yes, it is the right deck for you!

HOW TO TAKE CARE OF YOUR CARDS

Your cards should never be used as a game or a toy. They represent sacred symbols. Never let anyone play with or use your deck. Do not lend them out. Your friends will touch them as they're shuffling and choosing cards for you to read; that's okay.

Your energy is intertwined with the cards once you claim the deck as your own. Anyone else's energy could lessen or dampen the effect the deck will have for you in your readings. When you are not using the deck, wrap it in silk, cotton, or another natural fabric. Some people keep their deck in a wooden box.

TO PREPARE FOR A READING

Before giving a reading, I suggest you set the stage or create the right mood. Some people will burn incense or a candle. Others play soft, flowing music to create a relaxed atmosphere. Before beginning a reading, I always envision a beautiful white light surrounding me and the person I am reading for. The white light is a light of protection and peace. Some say a little prayer. Your mind should be clear and relaxed. You should never give a reading when you are upset, angry, tired, or in a bad mood.

HOW TO CUT THE CARDS

You will want to shuffle your cards first. Cut the deck with your non-dominant hand into three piles. Then pick up the piles, put them together (in any order), and fan the cards out on a table. Some readers just fan all of the cards out on a table and mix them up. Then they'll choose cards they are drawn to from the deck.

Other readers shuffle the deck like an ordinary deck of playing cards and fan them out. The client picks cards they are drawn to. Both ways are fine. One is no better than the other. This boils down to personal preference. Choosing the cards you want to read is important. You should take great care and not hurry to choose your cards. Take your time, slow down, and breathe! Run your hand over the cards, and see which cards draw energy to you. Which cards are calling to you? These cards are the ones you should pick up. These will have special and deep meaning. When you choose the cards, pick them up with your left hand if you are right-handed. If you're left-handed, use your right. This is a magic moment. Choosing your cards is almost like a ritual. If you honor the process, your reading will be accurate. The cards will honor you.

There are just as many layouts as there are tarot decks. We will only concern ourselves with three of them right now. The easiest one to use is the Yes/No reading.

YES/NO READING

The simplest way to get an answer using the cards is to ask a yes or no question. Shuffle the cards and think of your question over and over in your mind. You can ask it out loud if you wish. After you shuffle the cards, fan them out on the table and pick up one card that you are drawn to. If a card drops out of the deck while you are shuffling, you should read that one.

Ask a question that can be answered simply. Do not attempt to ask a long one that will require a detailed answer. Those types of questions can be saved for the longer layout readings. Phrase your question like this:

Will I be dating someone this year?

Will my grades improve?

Will I get a car?

This reading will not give you times when things are likely to happen. Do not ask the same question over and over, even if you do not like the answer. Do not ask the question twice in a twenty-four-hour period. Accept the answer, and decide what are the best steps you can personally take to deal with what the card has told you.

After you have drawn your card, look up its meaning in the next several pages. You will be able to determine if the card is favorable or unfavorable. For example, if you were to ask the tarot, "Will I be dating soon?" and you drew the Lovers card, the obvious answer would be yes, a new relationship is on the way.

THE THREE-CARD SPREAD (PAST, PRESENT, AND FUTURE)

Another simple layout you can do is the Past, Present, and Future reading. Shuffle the cards, fan them out, and pick three cards. The first card you pick should be laid to your left. It represents your past, what has already happened, what you know to be true. The second card you draw is to be placed directly in front of you. This is your Present card and it deals with current conditions and circumstances around you right now. The third card is placed to the right and it will tell you what you can expect to happen in the near future and the outcome of the event or circumstance.

This layout is good for timing events and if you wish to do an in-depth, longer reading. Shuffle the cards, fan them out, and pick twelve cards. The first card you draw should be the first one you read, and so on.

Place six cards in a row and six cards in another row beneath the first set, all facedown. Turn the first card over. This card will tell you what is likely to happen during the current month of the reading. Read the information on this card in the following pages.

Flip the second card over. It will tell you what to expect next month. The third card will give you insight on three months from now, and so on.

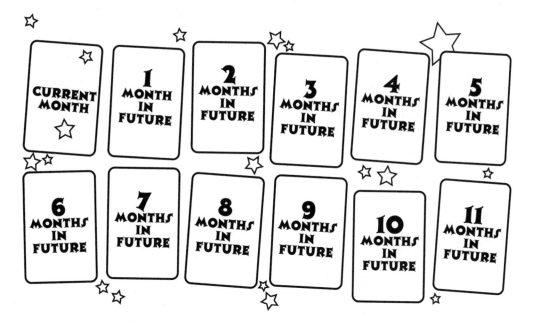

DON'T BE A FOOL!

Now let's look at the meanings of the cards.

The deck is divided into parts: the major arcana and the minor arcana.

MAJOR ARCANA

0. THE FOOL

I. THE MAGICIAN

II. THE HIGH PRIESTESS

III. THE EMPRESS

IV. THE EMPEROR

V. THE HIEROPHANT

VI. THE LOVERS

VII. THE CHARIOT

VIII. STRENGTH

IX. THE HERMIT

X. THE WHEEL OF FORTUNE

XI. JUSTICE

XII. THE HANGED MAN

XIII. DEATH

XIV. TEMPERANCE

XV. THE DEVIL

XVI. THE TOWER

XVII. THE STAR

XVIII. THE MOON

XIX. THE SUN

XX. JUDGEMENT

XXI. THE WORLD

0. THE FOOL

UPRIGHT POSITION

If the Fool falls upright in one of your tarot layouts, it means you can expect a brand new cycle of your life to begin. Perhaps you are starting a new school, graduating, joining a new group, or getting a job. You will have doubts about a new direction, but don't worry, things are likely to turn out in your favor. Just remember to trust your inner voice. This is an exciting time, but it can also bring unexpected challenges. You may be faced with a decision to make. However, you must take risks in order to get ahead and

succeed. In love, there could be a relationship on the horizon. In the job market, take a leap of faith and apply for a top position. It's kind of scary going out into the world, but you can do it! Try some new things and you will be pleasantly surprised!

REVERSED POSITION

The meaning of this card in the reversed position warns you must not proceed with current plans. You need to stop and analyze what is going on in your life. You could be taking the wrong road or making foolish decisions. There will be confusion. Do not rush into anything, for problems may arise that you do not expect. You will long for excitement or change, but your current choices are not the right ones. Be cautious; play a waiting game.

I. THE MAGICIAN

IL MAGO
LE BATELEUR

THE MAGICIAN
EL MAGO

DER MAGIER

DE MAGIËR

UPRIGHT POSITION

The Magician represents the power of your imagination. You have great ideas and inner power to manifest your own destiny. This card shows up when you are creating a new idea or opportunity in your life. You will be filled with enthusiasm and will learn to master new skills. Any project you are starting goes well. Like the magician, you have extraordinary powers to make your dreams come true.

REVERSED POSITION

There could be someone around you who is two-faced. Beware of so-called friends; they could be hidden enemies. You may feel tired or confused. Do not bow to peer pressure, but listen to your own inner thoughts. Stay true to who you are and things will work out for the better. There may be a few missed opportunities because you lack self-confidence. This troubling time will pass. You need to learn to trust your own instincts more.

UPRIGHT POSITION

The High Priestess will show up in your reading when you need to develop and trust your own psychic powers. She could also be warning you that a situation is not what it appears to be. There could be deception around you. You may have more dreams now. They could have prophetic meanings. Write these dreams down; take them seriously. Your subconscious mind is trying to get your attention. If you have a question or a concern that you just can't seem to resolve, it may take a month until all of your answers will be revealed. You must practice patience until then.

REVERSED POSITION

You may feel as if you are on an emotional roller coaster ride. You need to stay calm and not overreact to situations. Do not act quickly or impulsively right now, because you may regret your actions later. There will be friends and family members pushing your buttons. Remain cool, calm, and collected.

III. THE EMPRESS

L'IMPERATRICE
L'IMPERATRICE
III
THE EMPRESS
LA EMPERATRIZ

DIE HERRSCHERIN   DE KEIZERIN

UPRIGHT POSITION

You're coming into a period of great personal achievement. You will have lots of luck in relationships, at school or work. Projects that you begin now will flourish and grow. At work, your boss will notice your abilities. Your love life is fantastic! You will look and feel good. This is a pregnancy card too, so someone you know well could have a baby!

REVERSED POSITION

You may feel as if you have hit a road block. You're working very hard to achieve something, but nothing seems to be moving forward. This is a frustrating period. If you draw the Empress card in this position, it is important that you keep believing things will turn out for the best. Don't give up; have faith.

IV. THE EMPEROR

UPRIGHT POSITION

This card will give you great wisdom and insight to your question. You can achieve a great deal of success now. Move forward with courage and conviction. Doors will open easily. If you are looking for love, this card foretells of a new romance right around the corner. Your dreams can become reality, especially if you are willing to work hard for your goals and be open to new opportunities the Emperor wants to bring you.

REVERSED POSITION

Feeling down or discouraged about something? Probably. You may even feel like giving up! There are people around who won't give you a break. You may apply for a new job and not get it. You may ask someone out for a date and be turned down. There could be danger, frustration, and jealousy around you. You'll be learning a great deal about your own strength and what you are made of!

V. THE HIEROPHANT

IL PAPA / LE PAPE / V / THE HIEROPHANT / EL PAPA

DER HIEROPHANT / DE HIÉROFANT

UPRIGHT POSITION

If you are in search of an answer to a major problem, this card is telling you to take things slow. You need to create some sort of discipline or order in your life so things will run more smoothly. Stay with a regular routine; don't veer too far off the beaten path. Rather than argue, fight, worry, or be anxious, take the time to listen, to be quiet, perhaps to meditate. Your answer will come from deep within you. If your question is about love, you need to make more of a commitment with someone or break off the relationship. At work, you need to get promises in writing. This card is also telling you to get more rest. Go to bed earlier.

REVERSED POSITION

When reversed, this card means chaos and problems. You want to break free. You are tired of being a goody two-shoes. Life seems so boring! Friendships and relationships may be in turmoil. You may be attracted to the wild side of life. Be careful, you could be stepping into dangerous territory.

VI. THE LOVERS

UPRIGHT POSITION

When you draw this card, either a new relationship is coming into your life, you are in one, or you need to make a decision regarding love very soon. Your intuition will be strong and you will be using your heart rather than your head to make these decisions. Sometimes an old flame returns. You will feel strong emotions toward someone. A new love affair may lead to a serious commitment.

REVERSED POSITION

The Lovers card reversed means you will be going through a difficult period in your relationships. You may have to make a choice you don't want to. There will be rocky times ahead. Yes, there could be a break-up, tears, and sorrow.

DON'T BE A FOOL!

VII. THE CHARIOT

UPRIGHT POSITION

If you draw the Chariot, it means you are in a period of change. You may have been struggling with a situation in your recent past, but now you will have the freedom to move forward. You should have learned a great deal in the past several months and now realize that nothing is black-and-white. Nothing stays the same. This is a cycle in which you are moving away from the past and into the future, possibly new friends, new jobs, a new school, maybe even a major move. You will succeed now.

REVERSED POSITION

If you're traveling or are considering a trip, there may be delays or confusion. You may be lacking in self-confidence at this time. There are people around you who are trying to control you. You need to be calm and silent. Do not make any major decisions now; just sit and listen. This period will pass in a few weeks.

VIII. STRENGTH

UPRIGHT POSITION

You will be able to solve any problem that comes your way if you use a gentle touch rather than force. Be kind and gentle in your dealings with friends and family. Love is ever-powerful. It can heal all. This card is also telling you to love yourself. Treat yourself now. You probably have been busy with school, homework, practices, and chores. There isn't any time to rest. Slow down a bit! You can gain much strength and wisdom at this time. Your confidence levels will improve, and if there are any difficult people around you, they will be nicer.

REVERSED POSITION

You may not feel well. This is a period of low energy and for catching a bad cold. You probably need more rest. If you're burning the candle at both ends, exhaustion will set in. Try not to overdo it and go to bed earlier!

DON'T BE A FOOL!

IX. THE HERMIT

L'EREMITA
L'ERMITE
IX
THE HERMIT
EL ERMITANO

DER EREMIT
DE KLUIZENAAR

UPRIGHT POSITION

When you draw this card, you have just come out of a period of much activity and now it's time to stop and rest a while. If you are seeking an answer to a problem, you will not get it right away. You are supposed to retreat for a while, think it over, and then the answer will come. The Hermit represents your inner self, and by getting in touch with your inner being, answers come easily and light your way. It would also be wise to see a therapist or school counselor at this time.

REVERSED POSITION

The Hermit reversed warns you to be careful. Be cautious in all of your dealings. There are important messages all around you. Your inner voice is trying to talk to you. Your friends, teachers, and parents are giving you good advice. Heed it! You could feel angry now and reject any offers of help, even from your best friends. Take time to look at the other side of the coin. Things will improve shortly.

UPRIGHT POSITION

The Wheel of Fortune means you have ended a major cycle in your life and will soon start another one. You are especially lucky now. Things will fall in your lap. Be open to trying new ventures. You will be amazed at all of the wonderful opportunities that lay before you! The Wheel is turning in a good direction. Trust that everything will turn out wonderful and be for your highest good.

REVERSED POSITION

You will feel as if you are going backward. Nothing seems to be moving forward. You feel as if a dark cloud is hanging over your head. There will be delays and frustrations, but things do not stay this way for long. Know that this is a temporary position and things will start moving forward again. This is not a favorable time for starting anything new.

DON'T BE A FOOL!

XI. JUSTICE

UPRIGHT POSITION

You will find things fall in your favor easily. You are being instructed by this card to act with honesty and fairness in all of your dealings now. Whatever you put out will come back to you! Sometimes this card represents a marriage, a new relationship, or a wonderful friendship. There may be legal concerns at this time, but don't worry. Things will turn out okay.

REVERSED POSITION

People will not treat you fairly. You may feel like a victim and you probably are. You will notice people are working against you rather than with you. On a mundane level, this is a time to be careful with getting traffic tickets. Avoid after-school detention and suspensions. You could also work hard on a school project and not get a grade you deserve. Some things will seem unfair. Friends will argue more. You will desperately try to restore some peace and balance in your life right now.

UPRIGHT POSITION

This is a period in which you could experience sadness or sacrifice. You may have to let someone go or give up something you thought was important. However, it will not be as bad or as frightening as you think. You could also feel in "limbo," waiting for something to happen. Doing creative work such as art, writing, and music can help you get through this confusing time.

REVERSED POSITION

This card in the reversed position is actually a good thing! It means there is an end in sight for your frustration, suffering, or crisis. A lot of your questions will be answered. You do not have to go to great lengths to see changes now. You do not have to give up anything. You are free!

DON'T BE A FOOL!

XIII. DEATH

Special note: People mistake this card for meaning a physical death, as in someone close to them is dying. They look frightened if they draw it. They feel it is the worst card to draw in the entire deck. Some people even think the card means they will die! Not so. Death means the breaking down and rebuilding of something. There is a major change coming, but look at the sun beyond in the distance. There is good coming.

UPRIGHT POSITION

The Death card means a positive change. You will be letting go of old, worn-out habits, negative friends, and situations. You will start a new life or new direction. Thoughts and beliefs will change. Even though you may go through a period of self-doubt, so many new and wonderful opportunities await. Press forward; let go of the past and be open to what the future will bring you. There will be much happiness.

REVERSED POSITION

The Death card reversed means there will be a "block" in your life that you can't seem to overcome. You may be the cause of the blockage, or you may not want to let go of something or someone that is negative. Sometimes we suppress our feelings. We hang on to our old beliefs and negative thinking. You could be afraid to let go of a negative group of friends or an addiction. Fear will hold you back. Be more open and things will change for the better.

XIV. TEMPERANCE

UPRIGHT POSITION

You have recently gone through a period of turmoil and hard work. You are now open and ready to receive the good things the universe can offer. If something seems to be missing in your life, or if there is a feeling of emptiness, soon you will feel lighthearted and filled with joy. When you draw this card, you can land the perfect job, discover new friends, and even meet your soul mate! If you were depressed in the past, there was a reason for it. So you've reached this point in your life and can appreciate what the

world has to offer. Your life will be in perfect harmony and balance very shortly.

REVERSED POSITION

This card reversed means there is no balance in your life right now. You are so busy you can't focus. It's as if you are trying to accomplish too much too soon. Therefore, nothing gets done. You're headed for a major burnout. This could be a difficult time and you will be tested, but these tests will make you stronger. The way you look at life and your belief system may change a lot too.

DON'T BE A FOOL!

XV. THE DEVIL

UPRIGHT POSITION

You will be obsessed with a situation or someone. This is not healthy. You could also be a bit frightened too. Many times, this fear comes from being obsessed and not wanting to let go. Perhaps you are dating someone and are fearful he or she will break the relationship off. You may know this is for the best, but are so taken by him or her, you hang on to a dying love affair out of desperation. You could be too obsessed with making money and take on more jobs than you can handle. This card is here to tell you that true happiness comes from within. You could make a wrong choice if this card comes up in the spread. Do not misuse any powers of manipulation, as they may come back on you.

REVERSED POSITION

The reversed Devil card is good. It means you are free! You may have just went through a struggling period and come out a winner. You will no longer be held back or kept a prisoner. You can walk away from a bad relationship or a friendship gone sour and feel confident there will be good times soon; lots of laughter and fun!

XVI. THE TOWER

UPRIGHT POSITION

Expect the unexpected to happen. The Tower card represents dramatic and amazing changes in your life. Things could have been building up over a period of time to create a major explosion. The actual change will happen quickly. You could break a relationship off, quit a job without giving notice, or have a blow-up with your best friend. There will be some upheavals in your life. Watch out for stress and anxiety soon. After the dust settles, you will see clearly why this chaos had to happen. There are lessons to learn.

REVERSED POSITION

Expecting someone new to come into your life? You know a change is coming, but not sure when? The reversed Tower means yes, there is an upheaval, but it is expected and you can accept and manage the outcome well. There could be more surprises and twists and turns over the next few weeks, but you'll be able to handle them. This could actually be a very productive phrase of your life. Be open to accepting these changes. They're usually for the better.

XVII. THE STAR

UPRIGHT POSITION

There are new adventures coming into your life. You will be eager and hopeful about your circumstances now. Things will change for the better. Expect good to come to you. Friends will support you now. If you need help in any area of your life, do not be afraid to ask, because many will want to help. Doors open up; there are new opportunities like never before. You are being recognized and adored! This is a great card for showing off your talents and abilities too!

REVERSED POSITION

The Star reversed means you are full of indecisiveness and doubt. You have lost all faith in yourself. You are not ambitious and feel as if life is meaningless. This is a temporary state of mind. The best thing to do is to meditate, use uplifting affirmations, and just wait. This dark cloud will lift, but you must push yourself to keep going. You have a choice to either smile or frown. If you smile, the light within you will glow and things will turn around. Do not allow yourself to get down.

XVIII. THE MOON

UPRIGHT POSITION

Your sixth sense is heightened and you could be extremely psychic. This card also means you are tired and overwhelmed by life. There could be deceitful people around you; don't trust everyone. There's a lot of rumors and gossip too. The moon's phases last one month, so expect changes to occur in the next thirty days. You will need all of your energy to deal with the negativity. Listen to your intuition and get readings from others as it may be hard to interpret all of your dreams or visions at this time.

REVERSED POSITION

You will feel more at ease soon. There is less deception around you now. The ups and downs of life are coming to an end. If someone was lying to you in the past, you will be able to see this person's true colors clearly. You are no longer in the dark, so move forward with a clear conscience and determination. Don't let anything stand in your way.

DON'T BE A FOOL!

XIX. THE SUN

UPRIGHT POSITION

The sun is shining upon *you*. There will be success and fulfillment. You need to take the first steps to achieve goals now. If you have a new project or idea, go for it! You will feel a sense of rebirth and a burst of energy. You cannot fail! The world is waiting for you and granting your every wish and desire. Use this time to make progress and make changes.

REVERSED POSITION

You may feel defeated now or sometime soon. A goal or project you have been working on doesn't turn out as you had hoped. Someone else may bask in your limelight or get more recognition. Your time is coming, but not right now, so you need to keep the faith. Avoid getting depressed or involved in negative thinking patterns.

UPRIGHT POSITION

The Judgement card is a final decision card. You will make up your mind about something. Even if there have been difficult times in the recent past, much progress can be made now. The choices that lie before you are quite clear. Great changes can occur if you are willing to release old fears. Nothing is impossible now if you draw this card.

REVERSED POSITION

You could feel disheartened and discouraged. You may feel as if the dream you are chasing is not within your reach or the road you're on is leading nowhere. You may indeed have to change your ideals and goals now. Don't let negative thinking hold you back. There is a reason and a season for everything.

XXI. THE WORLD

UPRIGHT POSITION

This card means you have come full circle. You have gained a lot of wisdom while achieving a great goal. You'll be expanding your horizons now, perhaps graduating, getting a promotion, and meeting new people. You have matured and are ready to take control of your life and all the world has to offer. This is your "dance of life" card. The opportunities are endless as you enter this new phase.

REVERSED POSITION

A cycle of your life is coming to an end, but before this happens, you will experience frustrations and delays. You really don't want to make changes now, but you must. You could be going off to college and get homesick. There may be a sense of loss about a friendship or a romantic involvement. Change is necessary. You have to go with the flow whether you like it not.

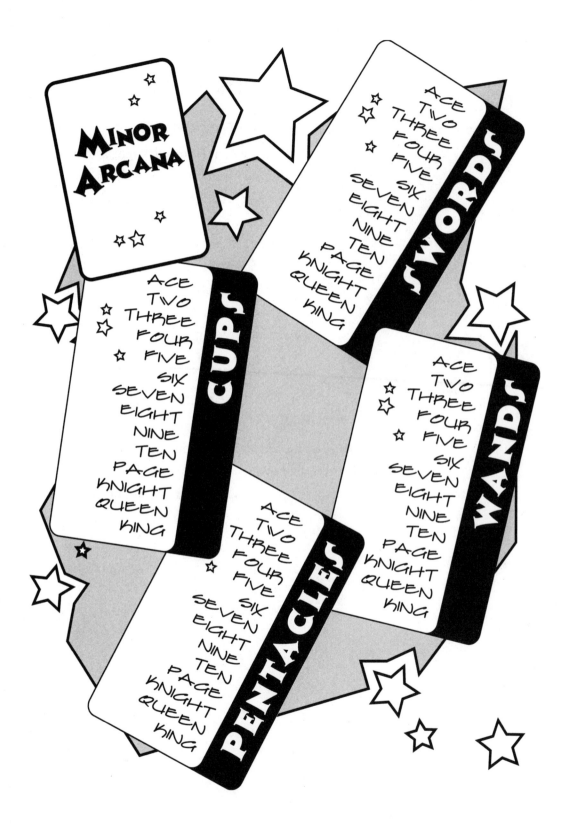

ACE OF CUPS

UPRIGHT POSITION

There's a new relationship right around the corner—but the Ace of Cups only shows you the potential of a relationship, not the result of it. If you find yourself attracted to someone, it's up to you to make the first move. This is a very spiritual card. So, listen to your inner voice to guide you when it comes to making decisions regarding matters of the heart.

REVERSED POSITION

There could be turmoil and upsets in your love life. Perhaps you are feeling very alone and withdrawn. Don't allow yourself to indulge in pity parties. Keep the faith and meditate often to find what it is you are supposed to learn during this somber time.

UPRIGHT POSITION

This is the soul mate card. When you draw it, you are on the verge of meeting your soul mate and a destined relationship is coming. You will soon share a special bond with someone whose love is unconditional. Be very aware of who has recently appeared in your life and be open to those yet to come.

REVERSED POSITION

There are problems ahead in a close relationship, possibly because one of you is acting foolish and immature. Even if your relationship seems stable, it is vulnerable and has the potential to fall apart. Tread carefully now, and don't cause any arguments or upsets that you'll come to regret.

DON'T BE A FOOL!

THREE OF CUPS

UPRIGHT POSITION

There are happy, joy-filled times ahead. You'll be working with lots of creative people and feel like part of a team. There's a wonderful party to attend and a reason to celebrate. Enjoy your successes as there will be many. Close friends are happy for you too. Include them in your plans. The Three of Cups signifies birthdays, weddings, showers, and all sorts of celebrations.

REVERSED POSITION

Count your blessings and be thankful for what you have. Don't envy other people's success, because yours is only delayed in coming. You may feel as if nothing exciting is happening to you right now. Life is boring. Try to express some joy for a friend's happiness. Your time is coming.

UPRIGHT POSITION

When the Four of Cups appears in your reading, there's a warning to heed. You have much love in your life, but if you take it for granted, that love can easily slip away. However, you do have the chance to recognize this and make positive changes, whether it be in your love life or friendship circles.

REVERSED POSITION

You may experience lots of disappointments in your personal relationships now. You are expecting too much from others. Be careful of a demanding or selfish attitude. This also could mean someone you are close to is acting arrogant and egotistical.

DON'T BE A FOOL!

FIVE OF CUPS

UPRIGHT POSITION

There could be a possible break-up or separation in a relationship, but there is still a ray of hope. You have time to change your course of action, to make things better and create happiness. It will take some work to overcome obstacles in love, but it can be done! Don't worry about things you can't change. Let go of the past; concentrate only on the future.

REVERSED POSITION

There is a sense of sadness that may take time to be overcome. There's a break-up in a close relationship. You will probably let it go. If you try and hang on, you are only postponing happiness. In time, you will see why this ending had to manifest. It is for your own good, even though you don't fully understand now.

SIX OF CUPS

UPRIGHT POSITION

You have recently gone through a time of despair in a relationship and are coming into a period of hope and happiness. There is a gift coming your way. Expect some pleasant and welcome surprises. All will be fine. You are moving forward and not allowing the past to make you a prisoner. The Six of Cups also suggests fertility, children, sex, and childhood. There is a new path to follow. Open your heart to the bright possibilities that await you.

REVERSED POSITION

You may feel as if you are stuck between the past and the present and can't move forward. You won't accept the gifts the universe wants to give unless you let go of the disappointment and sadness of recent weeks. There's a tendency to focus on the negative now. No longer should you look back—only forward. Take a chance and have faith that everything will turn out all right.

DON'T BE A FOOL!

SEVEN OF CUPS

UPRIGHT POSITION

You may feel as if you're playing *Let's Make a Deal!* This card appears when you have difficult choices to make. The cups are filled with wonderful but strange-looking gifts. You are being asked to choose among several options in your life now—all are tempting. In fact, temptation is the main theme in this card. You will make the right choice when you follow your intuition.

REVERSED POSITION

You may be tempted to go after a dream or ideal that is far-fetched and unrealistic. There could be other people who want to see you fail. One must think before he acts. Take time to consider and weigh any decisions. You may be tempted to make a wrong move, leaving yourself open to disappointment. Be careful and be on guard for people and circumstances that appear too good to be true. They probably are!

EIGHT OF CUPS

UPRIGHT POSITION

The past is gone. It cannot be changed. Look forward to the future. Relationships that ended are no longer valid. Someone new is coming into your life and wants to help you begin a wonderful journey. This is a period of self-discovery. You are being pushed to uncover your purpose and spiritual path. If you have let go of an old dream or goal, a new one is coming to replace it. You'll be very happy soon!

REVERSED POSITION

You may have to make some sacrifices now that you don't want to. Even though you may not understand why your current situation is in a state of flux, there is a reason for it. Now is not the time to act rashly or be impulsive. Trust that the universe is working with you on your behalf.

DON'T BE A FOOL!

NINE OF CUPS

UPRIGHT POSITION

This is one of the most positive cards in the entire deck. You will feel emotionally, physically, mentally, and spiritually at peace. The Nine of Cups is known as the Wish Card. Make a wish now and watch it come true. Give love and get it back threefold. Whatever your heart desires shall be granted. Rest assured you will get what you want, even though it may not be exactly as you expect.

REVERSED POSITION

You may feel as if your efforts are thwarted or blocked. Patience is the key in all of your dealings. Be extra careful of overindulging and getting sick. *Caution* is your key word now. If you overdo and take things to the extremes, you may suffer disappointments.

UPRIGHT POSITION

There is an abundance of peace and happiness all around you. You have recently completed a journey, a goal, or task. It was successful; now enjoy the moment. Your success is not fleeting—it will last. You are free to enjoy what the universe has given you. You may have found true love. If not yet, it is right around the bend. Both you and the object of your affection will be filled with the power of love.

REVERSED POSITION

Don't go looking for problems. You are undergoing a final test. You may feel as if you are making the same mistakes over and over again. There may be something you're not "getting." A sense of fear or failure may overcome you. You have nothing to fear. If afraid of pursuing a relationship or revealing your true feelings, you'll lose one of the best relationships to come your way in quite a while.

DON'T BE A FOOL!

PAGE OF CUPS

FANTE DI COPPE   KNAVE OF CHALICES
VALET DE COUPES   SOTA DE COPAS

BUBE DER KELCHE   BEKERS SCHILDKNAAP

UPRIGHT POSITION

When you draw this card, a very special person will soon make an appearance in your life. He or she is a true romantic at heart. He or she may be artistic and creative. This special person is here to help you grow spirituality and teach you about love and compassion. This new encounter may seem to have a fated or destined quality. Expect the unexpected when you draw the Page of Cups! Someone exciting is about to change your life!

REVERSED POSITION

You may experience bouts of depression and feel life is headed nowhere. The goals and hopes you had are fading and you can't seem to get excited about anything right now. This dark time will pass. Your subconscious is trying to send you messages, so be very aware of what your dreams are telling you now. Write details down if you can remember them in the morning. Don't give up; this is only a temporary setback.

KNIGHT OF CUPS

UPRIGHT POSITION

This Knight brings special invitations, marriage proposals, and messages of love. Sometimes the card signifies the beginning of a relationship. Other times the Knight merely means a new project, big event, or friendship is developing. If you meet someone under his influence, the person is likely to be a big flirt and very passionate!

REVERSED POSITION

You are getting too wrapped up in unrealistic goals. You may be blind to what is really going on around you. It is fine to go after your dreams, but do not become obsessed or you'll wind up on the losing end. In relationships, be wary of smothering a partner. You may wear your heart on your sleeve and could likely end up getting hurt. Be realistic, as your imagination may end up getting the best of you.

DON'T BE A FOOL!

QUEEN OF CUPS

UPRIGHT POSITION

This is one of the strongest tarot cards for psychic development. The only card that rivals its powers is the High Priestess. When you draw this card, you're being asked to tap into your intuitive powers and watch them grow! You are also a comforting figure to friends at this time. Giving advice and showing compassion to those you care about may take up quite a bit of your time. You can easily manifest things you desire now.

REVERSED POSITION

One could easily lose herself in daydreams now. Think with your head, not your heart. You may get too attached or dependent on other people, scared to stand on your own or make any decisions. You must create a balance between logic and emotions. Don't allow unjustified fears to take over. Things are not as intimidating as they appear.

UPRIGHT POSITION

The King of Cups is telling you to settle your affairs in a peaceful, loving way. There is a new relationship coming that is stimulating and inviting. Your new romantic interest speaks from his heart. He is romantic and kind. You can learn much from this person, so keep an open mind and listen to what the King has to tell you. If you need support on a project or dilemma, someone will appear to help you.

REVERSED POSITION

There is a man coming into your life who could be selfish and untrustworthy. He lies to get his way and is quite egotistical. In the beginning of the relationship, you may feel very drawn to him and in awe. But after time, his ulterior motives may be more evident and you could emotionally get hurt. Also during this time, you should not blame others for any failures or disappointments you may suffer. You yourself may have made poor choices and must own up to them.

ACE OF PENTACLES

UPRIGHT POSITION

There is fame and fortune coming your way! If you have been working on a specific goal, it will soon pay off. There's a turn of events in your favor, so get ready! Success is within your reach. The Ace of Pentacles also foretells gifts and proposals. Now is not the time to fantasize or dream about what you want to do—you must get out and make things happen.

REVERSED POSITION

There's a block to progress. One must not be greedy. Take the rose-colored glasses off and take a hard look at reality. You could be missing the boat. You are being instructed to look at your goals from a spiritual standpoint, not merely a materialistic one. Are these goals and desires for your highest good? If the answer is yes, proceed; if no, rethink your agenda.

TWO OF PENTACLES

UPRIGHT POSITION

There will soon be a major change in your life, most notably in the area of money. If you have been feeling bored lately, get out and have some fun! If you're studying or working all of the time, plan some downtime. Learn to "play" again. This card shows you will have several projects going at once. They could be school interests, sports, and hobbies, so plan your time wisely. This card gives you an opportunity to expand your horizons, and at the same time create balance in your life.

REVERSED POSITION

If you're not flexible or open to making changes, things could fall apart now. You'll feel broke and misunderstood. You may have too many things going and won't be able to excel in anything. Slow down; notice what's going on around you. If you don't create more of a balance in your life, you'll soon feel as if you're caught in the middle of a raging tornado!

DON'T BE A FOOL!

THREE OF PENTACLES

UPRIGHT POSITION

If you have been working hard, you will soon be rewarded. If there is a goal that truly inspires you, you'll achieve it. You feel excited about your future and fulfilled. You are mastering something right now. It could be a foreign language, a new skill, or a technique. This card tells us that with hard work and determination, any goal is possible.

REVERSED POSITION

When you draw this card, it is a warning that one must be very responsible now. You have to stick to schedules and routines. You should follow all rules and procedures. If not, problems prevail. Take a look at your current circumstances. Are you happy or discouraged? If you feel let down, get back into a daily routine and put more structure in your life.

FOUR OF PENTACLES

UPRIGHT POSITION

This card brings financial gain through other people. You may receive an inheritance, a raise in an allowance, or a raise on the job. Expect special blessings and gifts from others. You may have a birthday or other reason to celebrate. Look forward to rewards that are promised. Shopping for new clothes and updating your wardrobe may be a priority too.

REVERSED POSITION

You are being warned not to be greedy. If you act selfishly, you could actually lose money or benefits. You are in a period where you must be very aware of your motives. If you treat people fairly and are kind and giving, your life will prosper. If you act egotistical or arrogant, you may lose a good friendship or gain a few enemies.

DON'T BE A FOOL!

FIVE OF PENTACLES

UPRIGHT POSITION

This card is a warning that you are likely to experience a loss of some kind. It could be financial; it may be that a friendship is ending. You can stop it from happening. If you have already been dealt a blow, you do have the ability to change things for the better. You can rectify the situation; there is hope. Let your intuition guide you on how best to accomplish the task. It won't let you down.

REVERSED POSITION

There is a reversal of misfortune. If you've experienced a loss of any kind—whether it be financial, friendship, relationship, or recognition—things are turning in your favor. Stop worrying, because all will be well if you go within and listen to your intuition. A resolution to a problem is close.

UPRIGHT POSITION

You have grown much as a person over the past several months. You've come through a period of darkness and despair and now have much more faith. You are being called upon to help or guide other people, perhaps the less fortunate. Give of yourself, your newfound wisdom and compassion. Spend time with a friend who needs a shoulder to cry on. Remember, the best gift you can give someone you care about is your presence.

REVERSED POSITION

Someone is trying to help you, but you may not accept his or her generosity; take it. Others are offering you solid advice; heed it. This is not a period in which you should try and tackle problems alone. You need other people. Accept their offers of help. The law of karma is in effect now. Whatever you put out comes back to you. If you've helped others in the past, this is your time to receive. If not, you may feel alone and helpless.

SEVEN OF PENTACLES

UPRIGHT POSITION

A major accomplishment is yours! A difficult task has been completed. The best part of a goal is the journey and experience of getting there. Once you reach it, there could be a letdown. If this is what you are experiencing or feeling now, you may need to reevaluate your goals. You've won the game! You crossed the finish line. But what now? What's next? It's important to start a new game plan. Begin reaching for a new goal. You are not satisfied to rest on your laurels. You must take new risks so you don't become stagnant.

REVERSED POSITION

There has been a recent letdown. You may have not accomplished everything you have set out to do. You've felt you've been heading in the right direction all along, but someone else has blocked you. You need to step back and take a rest for a while, rethink some of your plans and strategies. After time you will see how quickly things move forward again.

EIGHT OF PENTACLES

UPRIGHT POSITION

You have been working very hard and seeing little pay-off. It will come. If you have shown dedication to a project and it is nearing completion, know that you will receive recognition and reward, but not until the bitter end. You may feel like giving up on a plan—don't. The Eight of Pentacles brings a guarantee of success, but only after you have passed all of the tests. If you have shown great commitment to a relationship, school, a project, or a goal, good will come from your efforts.

REVERSED POSITION

You need to listen to the advice others are giving you. There are blocks to your path of progress, and if you get discouraged and quit too soon, there is inevitable failure ahead. A master, teacher, or angel has been assigned to help you now. Please allow them to assist you. If you try to do things your way and fail to take good advice, there will be disappointments.

DON'T BE A FOOL!

NINE OF PENTACLES

UPRIGHT POSITION

You are coming into a comfortable, secure, and happy period. The choices you made recently are good ones. There may be a windfall of some sort in the form of an inheritance or large gift of money. Someone may buy you a costly item or pay a large bill. You may receive a scholarship if you apply for one. With extra money at your disposal, you should spend wisely and enjoy your newfound wealth. On a higher level, your sense of spirituality is expanding too.

REVERSED POSITION

There could be a loss of some kind. Safeguard your things. Don't lend out special items to friends as they could lose or damage them. You may be wishing for a special gift or money to buy something. These things may not materialize right now. So be patient, as time will bring you what is truly needed and for your highest good.

UPRIGHT POSITION

You possess many gifts and talents and are being asked to share them with others. Spread the wealth—not only in monetary terms, but with your intuitive talent. Spend time helping others. Teach a younger child a skill. Share advice and insight with a friend. Whatever you put out comes back to you threefold. You have recently gone through a learning process. Now it is up to you to use the knowledge you've gained to help others.

REVERSED POSITION

There is a danger of being too greedy and selfish. Don't forget about your spiritual wealth. If you become too materialistic, you may lose it all. Money isn't everything. Even if you are lucky financially now, be careful of making money your god. The universal law of money is that it travels in circles. If you spend or share it, it comes back to you.

PAGE OF PENTACLES

FANTE DI DENARI KNAVE OF PENTACLES
VALET DE DENIERS SOTA DE OROS

BUBE DER MÜNZEN MÜNTEN SCHILDKNAAP

UPRIGHT POSITION

You are on the verge of landing a wonderful job! There's some sort of promotion or good news coming. More than likely your bank account is growing too. There could be many opportunities dropping in your lap. You are ready to accept lots of responsibility now, and will work hard toward a goal. Look at all of the opportunities presented and see which will benefit you the most. A messenger brings you good news.

REVERSED POSITION

You must learn to take more responsibility now. There's a tendency to act immature or foolish. Someone wants something for nothing. Please use your common sense, as things that seem too good to be true probably are. Now is not a time to act impulsively or foolish. Things are not as they appear.

KNIGHT OF PENTACLES

UPRIGHT POSITION

One may soon have to take charge of a situation. There is a new task or project being presented to you. It will come unexpectedly. You should keep all promises and commitments you make. Act honestly in any dealings. Many respect you now and are looking to you for guidance and leadership.

REVERSED POSITION

You are feeling lazy and unmotivated, and because of this, you will lose out on developing new skills. Your reputation is at stake too. Keep all promises, no matter how big or small. Old worn-out modes of doing things are detrimental. Try new techniques if you feel blocked. Use your imagination for better results.

DON'T BE A FOOL!

QUEEN OF PENTACLES

REGINA DI DENARI   QUEEN OF PENTACLES
REINE DE DENIERS   REINA DE OROS

KÖNIGIN DER MÜNZEN   MUNTEN KONINGIN

UPRIGHT POSITION

This is the Mother Card. When you draw it, a special, maternal woman may be coming into your life to help with an issue or concern. Or it could be that you are "mothering" someone else. Whatever the case, maternal instincts are high. You will feel generous and kind. You have a direct link with a powerful spiritual energy. With devotion and a positive attitude, know that you can accomplish any goals you have set for yourself.

REVERSED POSITION

You may become obsessed with something or someone that is unhealthy for you. You need to value yourself more. If self-confidence and self-esteem are lacking, this is the time to give yourself a good talking-to. Stand firm in your beliefs and don't let discouraging remarks or failures keep you down. Stay out of pity parties and away from negative people.

KING OF PENTACLES

UPRIGHT POSITION

Everything you touch turns to gold! Part of the reason for your success is because you have laid good karma and a solid foundation. You deserve reward because of all the kindness and devotion you have shown to others. Expect good things to come your way now, and be open to expanding your interests and horizons. With the King of Pentacles here to help, you can't go wrong!

REVERSED POSITION

You could work very hard, only to discover that when you reach the top, your world comes crashing down! Don't get swept away in empty promises and foolish ideas. Someone, possibly a man who seems very wise, is giving you bad advice. You should not rely on others now. Don't expect too much to happen. This period will pass; it won't last forever.

DON'T BE A FOOL!

ACE OF SWORDS

UPRIGHT POSITION

You are in the beginning stages of a new relationship, project, or situation that can be perceived as either a very good thing or quite negative. You have great power within you, but if not used wisely, it could be taken away from you. There is a breakthrough in your current dilemma. Doors are opening for you; problems solved. This is a period in which you can break free from the past, self-doubt, and limitations. You have tapped into some great and potent power. Use it for your highest good.

REVERSED POSITION

Misuse and abuse of power is evident. When one tries to force his or her way or control others, often there is a loss. Someone may be trying to control or push you into doing something against your wishes. Don't fall for manipulation. If you are the one attempting to mislead people, it would be wise to understand the true motives behind your actions.

UPRIGHT POSITION

You may be feeling quite emotional now. There is a fork in the road or a dilemma you can't seem to solve. Your heart is battling your head. Try and keep your emotions in check. Action must be taken now, but you prefer to do nothing. You can't expect fate to intervene. It is you and only you who can make a decision. Think logically now. An agreement will be made shortly.

REVERSED POSITION

You have recently made a decision. Now the consequences of the decision are unfolding. You are able to move forward without hesitation. You are able to emotionally express how you feel. Stress and tension are moving away from you.

DON'T BE A FOOL!

THREE OF SWORDS

UPRIGHT POSITION

There is sadness around you, reason to cry or mourn. There could be a separation or a break-up in a romantic relationship. You may also feel sad over the loss of a friendship. Whatever type of relationship rejection you are feeling, there are tears. There may be quarrels and arguments. Sometimes this card represents surgery or dental problems.

REVERSED POSITION

This card reversed simply means your sorrow is ending. You are well on your way to a wonderful recovery. Your heart is still hurting, but indeed healing. The worst is over. There may be a minor surgical procedure pending.

UPRIGHT POSITION

You are in need of some downtime. Try a little R and R. The past few weeks have been stressful, and you need time to recharge your batteries. Plan a vacation or day trip. Anything you do to break from your regular routine will lift your spirits now.

REVERSED POSITION

There is no time for play. You're on the go! People make more demands and your schedule is hectic. Be careful of overdoing things, because your health could suffer. This is a time to catch a nasty cold, so try to maintain a balance in your life.

DON'T BE A FOOL!

FIVE OF SWORDS

SPADE
EPEES
5
SWORDS
ESPADAS

SCHWERTER
ZWAARDEN

UPRIGHT POSITION

Your ego could get out of hand. You or someone around you is acting in a destructive or selfish manner. People could be sabotaging your efforts. Watch out for sore losers and two-faced acquaintances. There's lots of gossip. You'll win the battles you fight, but they may cost you a few friends. Watch your tongue!

REVERSED POSITION

You are dealing with people who want to see you fail; trust no one. They are trying to lower your self-esteem. Don't put yourself in a position where you could be a victim. This is a card that foretells of enemies who will stop at nothing to get their way. This is not a time to fight battles you can't win, even if you believe in the principle of a matter.

SIX OF SWORDS

UPRIGHT POSITION

You are coming out of a period of darkness and limitations. Any stress and anxiety you feel is fading. Peace will soon
surround you. There is an opportunity
to travel long-distance. You may also be
taking new classes or changing schools.
Friends you haven't heard from in a
while may reappear in your life. There is
a feeling of tranquillity and calmness.

REVERSED POSITION

No matter how hard you try, you can't
get rid of the problems and troubles that
have been plaguing you for the past several weeks. No one is helping
you out either! You feel trapped. If you've planned a trip or an out-
ing, it could be canceled. This is the perfect time to face reality. If you
don't confront your challenges head-on, they will never go away.

DON'T BE A FOOL!

SEVEN OF SWORDS

UPRIGHT POSITION

Someone around you is being deceptive. There's a person you may trust who's lying or trying to cheat you. Be wary of all new acquaintances. Sometimes this card represents a theft, so safeguard your belongings. Stay clear of any schemes now, and don't get caught up in peer pressure. Be selective in your speech. Things you say could and will be held against you. Your reputation is on the line.

REVERSED POSITION

If someone has taken advantage of you or wronged you, everything will turn out in your favor. Many will offer assistance at this time. Do not feel sorry for yourself or act like a victim, because all will turn out in the long run. You will get credit when credit is due.

EIGHT OF SWORDS

UPRIGHT POSITION

This card means you are in a period or situation where you feel blocked, held back,
and restricted in some way. Whether you
recognize it or not, these are limitations
you placed on yourself. You are your own
worst enemy now. Face your fears; do not
let past hurts hold you back from creating
the future you seek and making dreams
come true. Be careful of little accidents at
this time too.

REVERSED POSITION

You can now break free of any chains.
Pressure is starting to subside and you are once again free to move
forward and make positive decisions. A roadblock is removed. You
clearly see what or who was holding you back and can work easily
around the situation.

DON'T BE A FOOL!

NINE OF SWORDS

UPRIGHT POSITION

This is the nightmare card. You are not sleeping well. Even when you are in a deep sleep, it is not a peaceful one. Worries weigh heavy on your mind. Your subconscious is trying to tell you something. Know that your worst fears or concerns will not likely materialize. You probably have come through a difficult period and are just suffering the aftermath emotionally. You may lose sleep now, but all will be fine.

REVERSED POSITION

Your nightmare is over! You still may have problems occur in your everyday life, but personal situations are improving. There is good news and hope on the way. Pleasant dreams resume as you no longer have anything to worry about. Don't allow your imagination to get the best of you. Expect good things to happen, and they will!

TEN OF SWORDS

UPRIGHT POSITION

You have hit rock bottom. You are giving up! There is an ending in your life, and you can no longer hang on to this losing proposition. One must let go! Nothing is working out as you had planned, and the only thing to do is rethink your plans. There is a sense of loss and sadness, but you must let go. You'll feel depressed for a while because this change has been forced upon you. Prayer or mediation will help you.

REVERSED POSITION

The worst is over. You can see a new day dawning. There are improvements and change for the better all around you. An old cycle of your life is ending and a bright, new one is emerging from the darkness. Many will want to be of assistance and help you now; accept their offers. You will be able to overcome any problems.

PAGE OF SWORDS

FANTE DI SPADE   KNAVE OF SWORDS
VALET D'EPEES   SOTA DE ESPADAS

BUBE DER SCHWERTER   ZWAARDEN SCHILDKNAAP

UPRIGHT POSITION

Be wary of gossip. Someone around you is trying to spread lies and manipulate others. These lies could be about you. Malicious rumors are spreading. There may be someone spying on you too. Unexpected problems surface with people you don't know all that well. A promise will be made and then broken. Be careful of whom you trust.

REVERSED POSITION

Any decisions you need to make must be handled with great care and given much thought. Do not act hastily, as you may not have all of the answers just yet. Don't sign any contracts unless you have someone you trust look them over. A younger person or sibling may cause you a great deal of trouble. Someone who is supposed to be a friend may prove to be otherwise.

UPRIGHT POSITION

Your emotions may get the best of you as an unexpected argument develops out of nowhere. There is fierce struggle or competition to be wary of; be strong now. Let your head lead rather than your heart. The Knight of Swords also foretells rash, impulsive behavior in romantic relationships. Don't say things you'll later regret.

CAVALLO DI SPADE   KNIGHT OF SWORDS
CHEVALIER D'EPEES   CABALLO DE ESPADAS

RITTER DER SCHWERTER   ZWAARDEN RIDDER

REVERSED POSITION

Do not start a new project or relationship now. It simply won't work out. Someone around you is trying to upset your plans or sabotage something you are working on. Without warning, there could be a breakup in a friendship or romantic relationship. There's a bossy and selfish person whom you need to stay clear of to avoid more trouble.

DON'T BE A FOOL!

QUEEN OF SWORDS

REGINA DI SPADE   QUEEN OF SWORDS
REINE D'EPEES   REINA DE ESPADAS

KÖNIGIN DER SCHWERTER   ZWAARDEN KONINGIN

UPRIGHT POSITION

Stand up for yourself. Be clear and concise in all communications. Go after what you want. Your career opportunities are strong if you know what you want. Romance is not favorable now, but job opportunities are. Make the most of this time and add to your bank account. There may be a woman around you who's experiencing a lot of grief. Be kind to her.

REVERSED POSITION

There is a vindictive, domineering, negative woman around you. She may force you to do things her way. If this woman doesn't get her way, she can be revengeful and mean. Stay clear of her if you can. She cannot be trusted and is very manipulative.

KING OF SWORDS

UPRIGHT POSITION

An important decision will be made that benefits you! A strong man, father figure, boss, or teacher will be on your side. You have a strong ally in your corner when you need him most. This card also represents original thinking, which helps you make strides in school or on the job. You may come in contact with lawyers, politicians, and professional men now.

REVERSED POSITION

Stay clear of bullies or people who want to use you. You may be deceived, intimidated, or treated unfairly in a situation. Someone may say something to hurt your feelings. If you have felt victimized, don't fight back as you'll end up losing more ground and self-esteem. Don't allow yourself to be put in situations where you could get hurt or taken advantage of.

ACE OF WANDS

UPRIGHT POSITION

You will be starting a brand-new venture. There is a new goal you hope to achieve. The energies that surround you now create more enthusiasm and faith than ever before. Go after your dreams! This is a period of real adventure. You can make things happen easily, as many exciting opportunities seem to drop in your lap. This is the start of something big!

REVERSED POSITION

No matter how hard you try, it seems nothing gets off the ground right now. So don't push or get discouraged. A promise may be broken. A project never gets off the ground. You'll feel frustrated and like giving up. Your efforts are thwarted. You may have lots of enthusiasm, but things won't fall easily into place. Bide your time until the power of the universe works with you once again.

UPRIGHT POSITION

You are on the threshold of a new project or a bright beginning. However, action must not be taken just yet. This is a waiting period. These early stages of development are important as you reassess your direction and redefine your goals. So don't look at this waiting period as a bad thing. Know your dreams will happen, but you need to get your ducks in a row before true progress can take place. Success will be yours through hard work and determination.

REVERSED POSITION

Things will not work out as you had hoped or planned. You'll likely lose interest in a project, so don't waste a lot of energy or time on something your heart isn't into. You'll feel as if you're driving down a dead-end street. Many disagreements and arguments occur. People you could count on in the past may not be there for you now.

DON'T BE A FOOL!

THREE OF WANDS

UPRIGHT POSITION

Any project or goal you started is coming along nicely. You may be in the beginning stages of creating or achieving something very special. There is a sense of fulfillment and enthusiasm as you work toward your goal. You can count on others for their support. You may get a new job. This card's influence also represents travel.

REVERSED POSITION

You are encountering many roadblocks now. There is adversity. No one will cooperate with you, and goals have to take a back seat to other matters that need your attention. This is a time to review and revise some of your hopes and dreams. Perhaps your expectations are too high. Rethink what you are doing and the path you're currently on. Make changes and set realistic goals that are not impossible to attain.

FOUR OF WANDS

UPRIGHT POSITION

This is a happy card promising you fulfillment and the attainment of your
goals. It's time to celebrate! There could
be a special invitation coming your way
too. Perhaps you are throwing a slumber
party or it's someone's birthday. Whatever the occasion, people are in a good
mood. This is also a time to consider
moving to a new home. Some will leave
for college soon or get their own place.

REVERSED POSITION

This card drawn reversed means the same
as the upright position, except success is not as grand. You will feel as if
you have reached a long-term goal, but only after a series of challenges,
difficulties, and hard work on your part. Nevertheless, you will experience some sense of completion. Sometimes this card represents a
deeper commitment or promise in a relationship, but not marriage.

FIVE OF WANDS

UPRIGHT POSITION

You are embarking on an exciting adventure or challenge. You must be up for the part. One should not act passive. You will achieve success only if you are ambitious and assertive. You will have many rivals. If you're concerned about a romantic situation, you must compete for another's love and attention. You are filled with energy. It's a good time to play sports or become involved in some sort of good-spirited competition.

REVERSED POSITION

People are not playing fair. If you're involved in any type of competitions—sports, the game of love, contests, etc.—know that you'll meet some very malicious opposition. Competitors will be manipulative and perhaps lie or cheat to win. Also, take better care of your health when this card is drawn. You could be burning the candle at both ends and need more rest.

SIX OF WANDS

UPRIGHT POSITION

Recognition and achievement is yours! You could receive a scholarship now or some sort of award at school. If working, a promotion could be near. All of your hard work and perseverance will pay off; problems disappear. There is much to celebrate; expect nothing but good news. Travel is on the agenda too.

REVERSED POSITION

You will see nothing but delay and defeat. If you are competing with someone else, it's likely the other person will win. You just weren't up to the challenge. If applying for a job, don't expect to get a call. If you're hoping to ask someone out on a date, wait! Now is not the time to move forward. Play a waiting game for a few weeks and try again.

DON'T BE A FOOL!

SEVEN OF WANDS

UPRIGHT POSITION

A heated or competitive situation is coming to a head. If you stand firm in your beliefs, and are fair yet forceful, you will succeed. Do not back down, even if you feel you can't win—you can! Do not give up. You will win if you continue to hold your own. Try to tackle challenges one at a time. You'll be able to make a successful job move now. This is a remarkable time for learning new things. You may be doing lots of writing.

REVERSED POSITION

You'll be filled with fear, but you must not quit anything you start. People may be angry with you, but probably will not confront you face to face. If you keep true to your path, you'll likely succeed. Beware of those who want to argue with you and lower your self-esteem. Don't allow others to walk all over you or wimp out.

UPRIGHT POSITION

You are moving forward at a fast pace. Your goals are in sight. This is an exciting time. Any efforts you make to promote yourself or to further a goal will go better than expected. Shoot for the stars; let nothing stand in your way. It's as if a path has opened and you can walk easily into a new venture. This is also a great time to start an exercise or diet program. An attractive love interest may waltz into your life, and new friends enter the picture too.

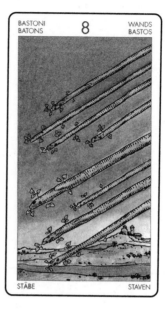

REVERSED POSITION

Everyone wants to argue with you. You can't seem to get ahead. No matter what you do, there seems to be a problem or an obstacle standing in your way. This is also the card that represents opportunities and incentives being cut off. You could be grounded a lot too. Watch your step!

DON'T BE A FOOL!

BASTONI BATONS 9 WANDS BASTOS

STÄBE STAVEN

UPRIGHT POSITION

This card is telling you to stand up for yourself now. You have to defend your position or belief system; don't waver. Be prepared for obstacles and roadblocks other people put in your path. Tackle challenges as they come along. Although you feel alone and overburdened, if you stand tough, success will be yours. If you back down, more problems lie ahead.

REVERSED POSITION

Your immune system is low and you could catch a virus or cold that's hard to shake. Learn to take better care of yourself. You are also in a weak position to succeed now. You have believed in something or someone that is not worth fighting for. Let go before you find yourself on losing ground. Any opposition you encounter now is strong—perhaps stronger than your defenses. Don't fight; the cause is not worth it.

UPRIGHT POSITION

Have you taken on too much responsibility lately? Do you feel as if you work overtime all of the time? You're closing in on the finish line. There will be reward and success. The Ten of Wands teaches you responsibility, willpower, and gives you drive to succeed. You're building great character during this period.

REVERSED POSITION

This is a positive position for the Ten of Wands. Pressure is lifting, and for the first time in a long time, you can see light at the end of the tunnel. You're able to put more fun into your life. Kick back and put your feet up. This stressful period is coming to a close and your life becomes yours again!

DON'T BE A FOOL!

PAGE OF WANDS

FANTE DI BASTONI   KNAVE OF WANDS
VALET DE BATONS   SOTA DE BASTOS

BUBE DER STÄBE   STAVEN SCHILDKNAAP

UPRIGHT POSITION

Looking for love? A new and exciting romance is right around the corner. You may find true love in your friendship circle. Start working out now, or sign up to play on a sports team. Healthy competition is highly favored. There is good news coming soon via the phone or e-mail. It could be a love letter from a secret admirer. You may get a call for a job interview. So make sure you're easy to get ahold of these days.

REVERSED POSITION

There's upsetting and disturbing news coming out of the blue. You could break off a relationship. Everyone is getting on your nerves. Expect petty arguments to arise out of nowhere. Make sure they don't become all-out wars! You could find yourself a little depressed and discouraged. Be careful of sharing secrets.

KNIGHT OF WANDS

UPRIGHT POSITION

Expect many positive changes to occur when you draw this card. You may be moving, going away to college, planning for the future, starting a cool job, or even starting a new romance. Someone who will play a very important role comes into your life. This person is here to help you become more successful, and has your best interests at heart. Listen closely to the wisdom he or she wishes to share. You may also plan a wonderful vacation.

CAVALLO DI BASTONI KNIGHT OF WANDS
CHEVALIER DE BATONS CABALLO DE BASTOS

RITTER DER STÄBE STAVEN RIDDER

REVERSED POSITION

There's a person around you who appears to be very charming, but in actuality cannot be trusted. This person makes empty promises. There could be instability in your job or your academic performance. Keep your grades up, as it's easy to fall behind in certain classes and homework now. If you are dating, there may be communication problems with your love interest that lead to mistrust.

QUEEN OF WANDS

REGINA DI BASTONI · QUEEN OF WANDS
REINE DE BATONS · REINA DE BASTOS

KÖNIGIN DER STÄBE · STAVEN KONINGIN

UPRIGHT POSITION

This card represents a career- or business-minded woman, or it could be that you are acting in a mature, professional manner. You may have a helpful, kind, and loyal female friend. She has your best interests at heart. Any venture you initiate or new project you are thinking about should proceed very well. A woman will help you along your path, and she is truly a benefit to have on your side.

REVERSED POSITION

A bossy woman may insist on getting her way. She could be a thorn in your side and a detriment to your plans. Be aware that someone may try to blackmail you or block your efforts. This card reversed also means to mind your own business. If you go sticking your nose where it doesn't belong, problems surface and you will be blamed!

KING OF WANDS

UPRIGHT POSITION

There is a strong, older man who will help you get out of a difficult situation. He may help you with money and/or give you a job. He wants you to achieve your goals and will help if you're willing to work hard. You're able to communicate well now, and your relationships should all run smoothly. This card foretells of new and exciting people coming into your life.

REVERSED POSITION

You will experience some deception soon.

There is a ruthless man who is a liar around you. Do not trust him. He enjoys being the center of attention, and may be using you for his own personal gain. Do not get involved in get-rich schemes, for you're surrounded by con artists. Learn to be more sensitive of other people's feelings, as you could let someone down.

DON'T BE A FOOL!

CHAPTER 5

WHAT COLOR "AURA" YOU?

READING YOUR AURA

Have you ever met someone for the first time whom you immediately felt comfortable being around? You immediately like the person. You have good, warm fuzzy feelings. Then on the other hand, there are people who make you feel uneasy to be around them. You can't wait to say "Adios" and be on your way! That's because some people drain your energy, while others add to it! These feelings happen because we are "sensing" another person's energy field, also known as an *aura*.

Think of an aura as a light fluffy cloud of cotton candy surrounding your entire body. It's invisible for the most part to the naked eye, but if you look closer, perhaps with your third eye, your intuitive, higher side will see it. You may think only psychics see auras, but that's not true. Everyone can see an aura if they know what they are looking for. You are already sensing them! That's the feeling described in the first paragraph. You sense other people's energy every minute of the day.

Let's say your friend comes over to visit. She's depressed about something. You'll sense it the minute she walks in the door. "What's wrong?" you ask.

"Nothing," she says.

"I know something is up with you! Tell me," you persist.

She finally gives in and tells you all about her problem. You sensed her energy was down before she said anything. Likewise, you will know when she is excited or happy about something too.

HOW TO DEVELOP YOUR AURA-READING SKILLS

First of all, you have to trust your intuition—that little voice in your head giving you messages or that feeling in the pit of your stomach. Clear your mind a little, take a few deep breaths, and slow down your thinking. Listen to what you "feel." What are the first thoughts that come to your mind? Notice how your body responds. Do you feel anxious, excited, confident, or like running away? It takes a little practice, but you'll get it.

This ability is something everyone has. Some people just use it more than others. Some are scared of it. There is nothing to be frightened of. Intuition is "how you feel." Once you get in touch with and trust those feelings, you'll develop and use them more and more. Don't question your first thought. The problem with intuition is most people try to analyze or second-guess it. Go with it! It won't serve you wrong. The more you use it, the more your psychic abilities grow.

You can use your intuition when reading your friend's auras. A lot of teens have told me they have been seeing colors around people for years, ever since they were small children. This is not unusual. If you are one of these teens who already see colors, you are seeing auras! So, let's take this task a step further. Let's learn how to read auras!

There is a simple way to read an aura. Have a friend stand against a plain white wall with no distracting pictures or curtains. Shut off the lights or make sure the room is dark. Take a flashlight and shine it above your friend's head. Be careful not to shine it in his eyes!

Concentrate on the middle of your friend's forehead between his eyes. Clear your mind. It may take a few seconds, but soon you should see soft, faint colors outlining his head, shoulders, and arms against the wall space. Sometimes the colors will be vibrant, sometimes they'll be faint.

The more you practice, the more you will see. Do *not* question it if you really saw a particular color. At some point, you will see a white light around your friend's body, as it's the most common color to have in the aura. He could have more than one color in his energy field, depending on what he is experiencing or feeling at the time.

An aura can extend for several inches outward from the body if one is open and energetic. If your friend is tired or sad, the aura is apt to be smaller, harder to see, and will hug his 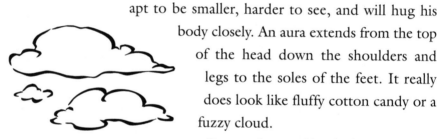 body closely. An aura extends from the top of the head down the shoulders and legs to the soles of the feet. It really does look like fluffy cotton candy or a fuzzy cloud.

Do you have a friend who makes you smile when you're down; a person who, just by hanging out with her, makes you feel happy and excited about life? This person is "extending" her aura. She probably has a large aura and is sharing it and projecting it on to you. Those who make you feel tired and depressed may have weak auras and take from your energy field. You may feel they are constantly pulling on you. You can't wait to get away from these people. Sometimes we call these people "energy vampires," because they suck the life out of us! We feel tired and drained when they are around. Most people don't mean to take energy and don't realize they are doing this.

When you're in love or are attracted to someone, you'll radiate the color pink. Have you ever told someone that she's "glowing" or perhaps "beaming"? These are words used to describe how an aura looks or vibrates. Sometimes you don't necessarily see an aura or color, but you feel it with your sixth sense. The feeling you experience means you're connecting with another person's energy field. Sound amazing? You do it all the time.

Kids and animals see and sense these auric fields much easier than adults. Their intuitive abilities are stronger because as we grow, our minds become so bogged down with mental and logical information, our psychic sense gets crowded out or ignored. When my daughter was three years old, I realized just how intuitive kids really are.

We were driving on a rural road and met my friend Cindy at a four-way stop. We both pulled over to chat. It was raining, and Cindy got out of her car to meet us. Her hair was wet, and she had no make-up on. She looked exhausted, tired, and pretty rough. But my daughter saw her aura and she exclaimed, "Mama, look at Cindy. She looks so beautiful!"

I said, "Yeah, right. Cindy looks like a drenched cat."

"No," she furthered. "Look at the pretty blue colors around her. Don't you see them? She looks so pretty!"

No, I didn't see them. I was too busy worrying about the weather. I didn't take the time to look beyond Cindy's wet head. But my little one did, and I'm glad she did. The blue that she saw was an odd blue I later came to learn. Blue usually brings a sense of peace and calmness to its wearer, but the blue my little girl saw around Cindy was actually a warning. Cindy later told us it was one of the death hues. Cindy almost died later that day. She is hypoglycemic and had a critical blood sugar drop. If she hadn't made it to the hospital, she would have died, according to the emergency staff. She would really have been at peace.

She has seen beautiful glowing blue auras around people right before they passed over. If you see blue around someone, it doesn't mean they are going to pass on. But if they are sick or have major health problems, it may be a sign to get them emergency care.

Someone who is ill or not feeling well will usually carry a gray aura. If I see gray in someone's energy field, I will visualize green or white to send healing. I will keep focusing and sending these colors until the gray melts away. If someone has just gotten over a bad cold, he may have gray and green in his energy field. This merely means the person is getting better and has plenty of his own healing power at his beck and call. If you notice a cold coming on, throw on a green shirt or a white outfit. It could aid in warding off the cold or speeding up the healing process. It is not a replacement for real medical treatment or advice, but it couldn't hurt! These are ways you can change your aura's colors just by using the power of your mind or choosing to incorporate certain colors in your wardrobe.

If you've had a bad break-up or a disappointment in your love life, wear pink—or better yet, "think pink." Pink is the universal color for love. It helps promote a loving feeling between you and someone special. Whenever I do aura workshops and lectures, I tell my guests to try the following experiment (many people write me or call to tell me it works!). If you are arguing with someone, or if someone is definitely acting in a disturbed manner toward you, visualize a pink light around that person. By doing this, you are sending the person loving vibrations. Even if you don't like the way she is acting or treating you, send her shots of pink color. You can think of a big light circling her body, or have it connect you to her like a pink string, from your heart to

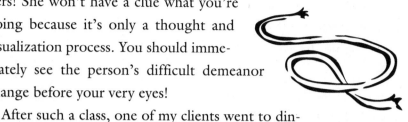

hers! She won't have a clue what you're
doing because it's only a thought and
visualization process. You should immediately see the person's difficult demeanor
change before your very eyes!

After such a class, one of my clients went to dinner. The waiter was in a bad mood and very temperamental
toward her and her guests. She visualized the color pink all around
the waiter every time he visited their table. She reported back to me
with much delight that his attitude changed in a matter of minutes.
He was laughing and joking and turned out to be a great server. "He
needed an attitude adjustment," my client said. "I gave him a big
dose of pink!"

You can do the same with testy friends and foes. If your teacher or
parents are giving you a hard time, and you can't seem to meet eye-
to-eye, think pink. You can even use this technique when someone is
physically far away. If your best friend is arguing with you on the
phone, just close your eyes and see pink all around her on the other
end of the line. This is a form of sending energy too, and it works
rather well.

There are times we feel a need to touch someone who is hurting,
either physically or emotionally. We are exchanging energy by choice.
Let's say your little sister fell off her bike and skinned her knee. You
would immediately go to help her and give her a hug. You're letting
your aura connect with hers so as to make her feel better! This is a
natural instinct.

We've all been around people who lose their temper from time to
time. I'm sure you are guilty of an occasional outburst too! Ever
hear someone say, "I am so mad, I'm seeing red!"? Besides being the
color of energy, red is also the color of anger. When a person gets

upset—very upset—his face turns beet red. All the blood rushes to the person's head. If you see this hue in someone's aura, it doesn't always signify he is mad. Before you jump to conclusions, take a moment to feel how you perceive it. Do you feel threatened by the person at this time? Do you feel excited or anxious? How about sexy? Red is also the color of sexual attraction. It's a sensuous hue. So if someone has a red aura, it could mean a few different things. Go with your first impression. Red mixed with other colors is good. It gives more energy and strength to them. But an aura that is entirely red or heavily cloaked could mean you have an "energy vampire" on your hands, someone who steals other people's energy. He could drain you too.

Have you ever been alone in your room and felt someone was looking at you? You didn't hear anyone come in, but you just sensed someone was there. Then you turned around and your dad was in the doorway. You're sensing his aura! You're feeling his energy.

Your aura changes according to what is going on around you. If one minute you are happy and energetic, and the next you hear some bad news, your aura can change in a split second. Even our thoughts can change our energy. Think about a sad movie. You'll feel tired or lose energy. Now, erase that thought and think about someone you really love or a fun trip you took. You'll feel the changes within you.

A trained eye can see the aura changing instantly! Remember, it can be of a single color or many different colors.

THE MEANING OF COLOR

There are many different colors that can show up in the auric field. They all have different meanings. Here's a list of the most basic colors you'll find when reading an aura.

PINK

Pink stands for love. If you see someone with a pinkish glow in his auric field, this is a good sign. This person is full of love and friendly vibrations. The person is feeling good and is open to giving and receiving love.

GREEN

Green is another good color to see around someone. It is a healing color. Many doctors and medical-field professionals have green in their aura. Green usually means someone is healthy and free from pain. If you see a heavy concentration of green around someone, it sometimes means that person was sick or endured pain but is now healthy!

BLUE

Blue is a color of peace and understanding. It has a calming effect. On a side note: if you can't sleep at night and you're tossing and turning, throw on a pair of blue p.j.'s or a blue blanket. Blue will help you relax. Don't wear red to bed. Red  is the color of energy and will keep you up all night! Blue usually means someone is relaxed and feeling pretty good about life. You'll feel at ease around someone with a blue aura.

YELLOW

Yellow is the color of communication. Yackety-yak! If you have a yellow aura, bet on a flurry of phone calls, creative writing assignments, letters, and e-mails. You'll be getting the latest gossip and talking up a storm yourself. Yellow is also good for mental concentration.

PURPLE

If you see purple around someone, it usually means she is very spiritual or her psychic abilities are developing and expanding. These people are looking for a higher purpose in life and seeking to find universal truth. They will be optimistic and positive. Purple in an aura can also mean lucky times are ahead!

RED

Red is the color of anger or energy. Red can mean a couple of different things. If you sense it in someone's aura, take time to "feel" it. Does the red feel good or bad? Someone with lots of red in his auric field will probably experience burnout down the road. But if red is mixed with other colors, it can intensify the positive energies of those colors. Red is also the color of sensuality. If you feel the red you see in an aura is too strong or it bothers you, that person may be guilty of stealing other people's energy. She may be angry too. Beware!

ORANGE

Orange is the color of joy! It brings energy and happiness. People with orange in their aura will make you feel alive and excited about life! They will find delight in simple things, and are a pleasure to be around.

GOLD

Gold is one of the highest spiritual colors you can have. Many psychics and highly spiritual people will have gold in their energy fields. Gold is usually intermingled with other colors.

GRAY

Gray is not a good color to have in your auric field. When I see gray in someone's energy field, I visualize a white light and a soft pink light around the person. Then I mentally visualize the healing color of green around her. I concentrate until the gray color has lifted or faded and turned into one of the brighter colors. Gray usually means the person is tired or sick. It's not healthy, and if in the energy field for a long period of time, it can really drag the person down emotionally.

WHITE

White is the white light of the divine, the power of protection. Most people have white in their aura. It is actually the first light to encircle their entire body. It brings peace, protection, and balance.

Besides the colors of an aura, you want to notice if the aura is balanced on all sides. The color should be even all around the body so the flow of energy is equal. Sometimes people's auras have holes in them. There may be gaps or breaks in the energy field. This is not always good. People who are ill experience this. A healthy aura is one that is fairly extended, vibrates in a positive color, and is balanced with no breaks in its path.

HOW TO READ YOUR OWN AURA

You've learned how to read auras and what the colors mean. However, reading your own aura can be quite difficult. There is a way to see it—through the help of a camera. Yes, your aura can be captured on film, but not with any old camera. There are professional aura photographers who will take your picture with highly developed and specialized cameras used just for this purpose.

These cameras cost about ten thousand dollars. Most can be found at New Age expos. Their prices range from ten dollars for a Polaroid snapshot to twenty-five dollars for a photo with a printed report and interpretation.

You will sit in a chair and place your hands on a magnetic armrest connected by a cable to the camera. That magnet will pick up your energy field and the camera will interpret it as color. Strike your pose, smile, and *poof!* the photographer takes your picture.

Like with a Polaroid, you'll have to wait a few minutes for the picture to develop. Then you will see colors all around your head, shoulders, and arms. The aura photos are usually just headshots or photos taken from the waist up.

Because your aura changes, so will the photos each time you have one taken. The colors in your picture will tell a lot about your emotional state—whether you are happy or sad, worried or excited.

I had one client who had a lot of problems with her mother. She came in to get an aura photo done at one of my psychic fairs. Her picture turned out all red, the color of anger. Months later she came back to get another photo taken. She had been in therapy for several weeks, and was working on emotional issues tied to her mom. Her picture still had red in it, but not as much.

There were also shades of blue (understanding) and green (emotional healing). Several months went by, and this young lady came back one more time to get another photo taken. She had finished therapy and was no longer angry with her mother. Her photo proved it! She had beautiful colors of blue, yellow, and a great deal of pink (love) all around her! The aura camera had captured her mood, emotions, thoughts, and feelings over the course of several months. It confirmed that she had worked through many problems and issues with her mom!

Auras can tell us a lot about how people are feeling, and perhaps even the issues they are dealing with. Now that you've learned a little more about the energy field, you can learn to use colors to help you feel better and boost your vitality. Remember, seeing auras is not difficult. Like anything, it just takes practice. I wish you all rainbows in your auric field!

CHAPTER 6

ROCKING YOUR WORLD

USING CRYSTALS

In the past several years, "power bead" bracelets have become very popular. They are the crystal or gemstone jewelry that attracts certain types of energy to its wearer. In fact, you may own several pieces yourself. The idea behind the power bracelets is really not new. For thousands of years, people have been using crystals to help draw and create powers of healing, love, protection, and prosperity.

Gemstones and crystals are part of nature's abundant creation. Crystals hold healing energies. These energies draw or vibrate to different things. One of the nicest crystals you can find for love and opening your heart chakra is the rose quartz. It is a soft pink color and helps heal broken hearts. It helps promote self-love too. If you're tired a lot, clear quartz crystal draws energy to you. It will give you that extra boost you need. Amethyst helps develop psychic abilities.

When you choose a stone or crystal, I suggest you follow your intuition. If a crystal warms up in your hand, its energy will work for you. If it remains cool or cold to the touch, it's likely the energies of that particular stone are not responding to you.

For years I have had a strong desire to find pink tourmaline jewelry. Not pink ice or garnet; even the beautiful pink sapphires would not do. I was drawn to the pink tourmaline. It is not the easiest gemstone to find. So whenever I ran across a ring or necklace with pink tourmaline in it, I bought it. I felt something was missing if I didn't wear the stone or carry it with me. There are different colors of tourmaline, but the pink is a heart stone that strengthens wisdom and willpower. It enhances creativity too. The energies the stone had to offer was something I needed at that time in my life. I don't wear the tourmaline as much as I once did, but often I find myself reaching for it at least once a week.

If there is something lacking in your life, or perhaps some talent or virtue you'd like to strengthen, carry a stone that enhances it. You'll likely notice subtle differences after just a few days.

There is another personal story I would like to share with you. About ten years ago, I was going through a difficult separation in my relationship. I bought a heart-shaped rose quartz pendant and wore it every day. I even slept with the necklace. Rose quartz, as mentioned earlier, helps heal broken hearts and draws love. I wore that stone for nine months until my ex came back into my life and wanted to work things out. The evening of our first date came and went. We had agreed to get back together. The next morning I realized my rose quartz necklace was gone! It was nowhere to be found. I searched high and low for the thing. The clasp to the necklace was strong, so I knew it didn't break off. I came to the conclusion the crystal had served its purpose and vanished. Its mission was completed; it played a part in bringing love back into my life. Other people have shared similar experiences they have had with their crystals vanishing into thin air.

Crystals can be used to create energy and to help with emotional balance. When you first buy a crystal, it is important that you cleanse it to make it yours. Since crystals absorb energy easily, you should release the energies of the other people who have touched it before you use it. I always place my crystals in salt water overnight. Never let anyone wear your crystals unless you want to carry their energy or issues around with you!

On the next page is a simple guide to enhance your life through the power of crystals.

GEMSTONE AND CRYSTAL GUIDE

TO ATTRACT LOVE

Rose quartz

Ruby

Pink calcite

Pink tourmaline

TO PASS EXAMS AND TESTS

Carnelian

Rhodonite

Green tourmaline

TO GET RID OF A COLD

Azurite

Jasper

Diamond

Ruby

TO HELP REMEMBER YOUR DREAMS

Garnet

Jade

TO CURE HEADACHES

Hematite

TO REMOVE NEGATIVITY

Jade

Opal

Clear quartz

TO INCREASE POPULARITY AND FRIENDSHIP

Barite

Turquoise

TO GET RID OF BUTTERFLIES IN YOUR STOMACH

Fluorite

Alexandrite

FOR LUCK IN SPORTS AND COMPETITIONS

Kansas pop rock (also known as Boji stones)

FOR SUCCESS WHEN GIVING A SPEECH OR PRESENTATION

Celestite

TO EASE DEPRESSION

Chrysocolla

Aventurine

Smoky quartz

TO BOOST SELF-CONFIDENCE

Bloodstone

Pyrite

TO RELIEVE FEAR OF HEIGHTS AND OTHER PHOBIAS

Aquamarine

Clear calcite

TO AID IN CREATIVITY

Yellow sapphire

Celestite

Blue sapphire

Amazonite

Blue topaz

FOR MONEY AND PROSPERITY OR A NEW JOB

Citrine

TO INCREASE PSYCHIC ABILITY

Amethyst

Lapis lazuli

Peridot

Blue sapphire

Opal

TO LOSE WEIGHT

Kunzite

Sodalite

TO HELP YOU SLEEP

Lepidolite

TO KEEP ENEMIES AWAY

Black tourmaline

TO HELP YOU RELAX

Amber

Blue lace agate

Fluorite

FOR STRESS REDUCTION

Onyx

Pearl

Blue topaz

Peridot

TO HEAL A BROKEN HEART

Emerald

Watermelon tourmaline

FOR MEDITATION AND HEALING

Clear quartz

Moonstone

Fluorite

TO IMPROVE EYESIGHT

Opal

GEMSTONES AND CRYSTALS
AND THEIR USES

Agate: Carry this stone with you when taking a difficult exam or test. It will help keep you focused. If you're finding it hard to tell the truth to someone, this stone will make it easier to fess up!

Alexandrite: If you are nervous about something, wear alexandrite. It will calm you and take away the butterflies in your stomach.

Amazonite: This stone gets your creative juices flowing. If you have a bad habit you'd like to kick, amazonite can help.

☆ AMBER

IF YOU TEND TO BE HIGH-STRUNG AND EMOTIONAL, THIS STONE WILL WORK WONDERS FOR YOU. IT'S KNOWN TO HEAL, SOOTHE, AND BRING HARMONY TO ITS WEARER.

Amethyst: This is February's birthstone, but anyone who wants to increase their psychic ability should wear it.

Aquamarine: Reduces nervousness. If you frighten easy or have a fear of heights, this gem will help dissolve those phobias.

Aventurine: Releases anxiety and fears. Wear it and you'll feel optimistic and happy!

Azurite: If you have a cold, carry this stone for a quick cure!

Barite: Your friendships and relationships will run smoothly with this stone.

Bloodstone: If a shot of self-confidence is what you need, carry a bloodstone in your backpack.

Blue lace agate: Soothes emotions and pain. It will help you to relax.

Calcite, clear: Helps overcome any fears you may have. By wearing this stone, you will know the difference between the truth and deception.

CALCITE (green)

RELEASES FEAR. IF YOU GET STUCK IN A RUT, GREEN CALCITE WILL HELP YOU TO COME UP WITH NEW IDEAS TO REACH YOUR GOAL.

Calcite, pink: Helps you let go of past hurts. Draws unconditional love to you.

Carnelian: Helps with grounding. You will feel more focused.

Celestite: If you are giving a speech or presentation before a group, wear this stone. It promotes creative expression.

Chrysocolla: Balances emotions. Reduces fear and anger. Helps calm an upset stomach. Eases depression.

CITRINE

CARRY CITRINE TO DRAW MONEY OR PROSPERITY TO YOU.

Diamond: This is a good healing stone. It intensifies the power of other stones.

Emerald: Works on all matters of the heart. When you're going through a break-up, or just on the outs with your best friend, wear emerald to heal your heart.

Fluorite: Good for meditation. Strengthens teeth and bones. Are you hyper? This stone will calm you down.

Garnet: Inspires passion and love. Sleeping with it helps you remember your dreams.

Gem silica: This is a rare and beautiful stone. It helps unlock your feminine side, and guys will get in touch with their feelings.

HEMATITE

IF YOU GET HEADACHES, THIS STONE COULD HELP RELIEVE THEM.

Jade: Promotes universal love. Radiates divine, unconditional love. Dispels negativity. Aids in dream study.

Jasper: A powerful healing stone.

Kansas pop rock: Need an energy boost? Grab a pop rock!

Kunzite: Used by many to kick addictions. Heals heartbreak. Enhances self-esteem and self-acceptance.

Kyanite: Helps with astral travel. Promotes truth, loyalty, and reliability.

Lapis lazuli: Increases intuition and spiritual growth. A stone of royalty. Brings past emotional hurts to the surface for healing.

Lepidolite: If you have trouble sleeping, put this stone under your pillow. It will help you drift off easily.

Lodestone: This is a magnetic rock. It realigns energy and auric fields.

Moonstone: When there's trouble in your love life, moonstone can help. It relieves frustrations and balances emotions.

Onyx: Relieves stress.

Opal: Absorbs negative energy and works with karma. Good for people who have eye trouble or wear glasses. Enhances intuition.

PEARL

SOFTENS PAINS. SENDS SOOTHING, PEACEFUL VIBRATIONS.

Peridot: Increases intuitiveness. Stimulates the mind, but reduces stress.

Pyrite: Gives you a more positive outlook on life.

Quartz, clear: The "everything" crystal. Magnifies the intensity of other crystals. Keeps negative energy away. Good for meditation and communicating with spirit guides.

Rhodonite: Take this stone with you to class if you've been up all night studying. It improves memory. It also dispels anxiety and confusion.

Rose quartz: The love stone. Vibrates love and draws love to you!

Ruby: A great love stone. Ruby promotes your zest and passion for life. It will help you fight off colds too.

SAPPHIRE (blue)

PROMOTES PSYCHIC ABILITY, CREATIVITY, LOYALTY, AND LOVE. HELPS WITH THE FLOW OF SPIRITUAL ENERGY.

Sapphire, yellow: Helps build creativity. Gives its wearer strength and discipline. Good for if you're working on creative ideas and projects.

Smoky quartz: Good for depression and fatigue. Enhances dream interpretation and channeling abilities.

Tiger's-eye: Softens stubbornness. Helps one to see both sides of the coin.

Topaz, blue: Promotes tranquillity and peace. Has a soothing effect on its wearer. Promotes creativity and self-expression.

Tourmaline, green: This stone will make your brain work better!

Tourmaline, pink: Heart/love stone.

Tourmaline, watermelon: The best heart healer.

Tourmaline, black: Offers protection from negative people and enemies.

TURQUOISE

A GOOD FRIENDSHIP STONE. GIVE IT TO SOMEONE YOU CARE ABOUT.

CHAPTER 7

WAXING MAGICAL

YOUR GUIDE
TO USING
CANDLE MAGIC

Would you like to learn how to create real magic? Do you wish to pass a tough exam? Perhaps make new friends? You can make wishes come true by learning the secrets of candle-burning. You can even stop gossip by burning candles; it's true. In the past couple of chapters, you've learned how color affects us. You've studied the use of gemstones and crystals. Now let's put this newfound knowledge to good use. Combine the power of color and crystals with candle-burning to create magic!

For centuries, people have been lighting candles while they pray for specific needs. Whenever anyone was sick in our family, my mother would light a green candle for healing. The person would feel better within hours. If she was short on money, Mom would burn purple candles. She'd light them to send energy out into the universe as she said her novenas to St. Jude. Money would come from surprise sources over the next few days, or she'd have a small winning on a lottery ticket. If there was turmoil in the family, she would light a white candle for peace and say her prayer to St. Joseph, the patron saint of families. Burning a candle to her meant giving her prayer or thought more spiritual energy.

My friend Sarah was devastated by a break-up with her boyfriend and burned candles for months. She created a loving energy and sent it out into the universe. Her target was her boyfriend. But the universe played a trick on her! Sarah's boyfriend Matt was really a jerk.

He had two girlfriends on the side, lied to her, and made a lot of empty promises. She took him back time and time again. No matter how emotionally abusive he was to her, Sarah believed he would eventually change.

After yet another difficult break-up and a confrontation with his other girlfriend, Matt took off. Sarah didn't hear from him for weeks. She heard rumors he had moved in with "girlfriend number three." This tenacious Cancerian gal wasn't about to give up. She knew she couldn't reach him on a physical level when he wouldn't return her phone calls, so she started burning pink candles every day. Pink candles are used to create more love in your life and draw a relationship to you. Little did she know at the time, but pink also helps create self-love, which was something Sarah needed after experiencing emotional abuse and a loss of self-esteem.

Sarah carved Matt's name on a new candle every day along with her own. Like clockwork, she burned the candle at the same time each day. She prayed that Matt and she would get back together. This went on for weeks, but Sarah never gave up. Then one day, magic happened! She went to the store, and as she pulled into the parking lot, a car pulled up beside her at the same time. She glanced briefly at the driver. It was Matt! He was smiling at her. All flustered and excited, Sarah got out of the car. Then, to her disappointment, she realized it wasn't Matt. This guy was the same height, build, and had the same blonde hair and blue eyes as Matt, but he wasn't Matt!

The young man spoke first, and the two started talking. Sarah was attracted him because he was a dead ringer for "the jerk."

When the guy introduced himself, Sarah almost fell over. His name was Matt too!

The good-guy Matt and Sarah are now married and have a baby boy.

The universe works in strange ways. The candles worked their magic, but not in the way Sarah had hoped. She got more than she bargained for. The new Matt is a great guy and very devoted. The intentions and energy Sarah put out into the universe by burning candles drew to her a love her heart and soul needed. Her prayers were answered. Magic happened, but for her highest good!

This story could have easily gone the other way, however. Sarah could have worked in a negative manner by trying to use controlling or manipulative magic, or sending out evil or bad intentions toward the old Matt and his other girlfriends. Then she would have gotten a negative response. But because she was praying for love in a positive and pure way, magically, a good Matt appeared to bring the type of love she so desired.

If you wish something bad on someone, or send negative thoughts out into the universe, it is likely the same will come back to you. Thoughts, intentions, curses, and evil practices are like boomerangs. That's why you should always pray or create magic for your highest good and that of others. Whatever you put out comes back to you—maybe not right away, but in time. This is the law of the universe. So create magic, burn your candles, say your prayers, and visualize a bright, beautiful life for yourself. It's not the candle that is creating magic or making a difference, it's your intention of thought, it's your energy. The candle is just a tool to help put that intention out into the universe. The flicker of the flame and the light gives your thought more energy, and energy creates action, thus producing an effect or end result.

There is really no time frame for magic to manifest. We may be impatient for a wish to be granted or an aim to be achieved. There is a time and place for everything. Just as you can't give up on a goal too soon, you can't get discouraged if things don't happen within a certain amount of time. However, if you continuously ask and pray for something, and you see no signs of getting any closer to achieving it, it may be time to reexamine your intentions. Are you asking for something that is really for your highest good, or just because you want it? Do you really need it? Would your desire hurt or hinder someone? Are your goals realistic? Say you want to be a famous singer one day, but don't bother to take vocal lessons. You aren't taking steps to create an opportunity for the universe to work its magic.

On another mundane level, whether you realize it or not, you create magic every day. The words you speak, the people you touch, the smile you share with a stranger—all the little bits and pieces of life make magic moments. Even life itself is magic. Know that you can create and manifest anything your heart desires if you take the proper action and if your will, intent, and purpose are strong. Burning candles give your thoughts more energy. So use this ancient practice for a pure purpose and all good will come to you!

The rules for candle-burning are simple. Buy a candle in a specific color for your need. Begin your prayer on the day of the week that's best suited to your intention.

My family was used to saying nine-day novenas, so we would burn our candles for nine days in a row for about an hour each day. Many people who work with candles burn their candles for seven days. This is the most common practice, so I suggest following this example.

To set up your candle rituals, you will need a nice, quiet area. You should burn your candles at the same time every day in the same room and for the same intention. You should use a new candle every day (you can buy cheap ones at the dollar store). Place your candle in a clear crystal, metal, glass, or wood holder, and make sure it is secure. Do not leave it unattended at any time.

Place a crystal or gemstone that corresponds to your intention's color near the base of the candle.

I suggest you burn your candles for one hour each day. If you cannot stay with them that long, burn them for at least ten minutes each day. Do not reuse your candles on the next day or for any other purpose.

As you light the candle, say your prayer or affirmation out loud. You can write your own affirmations and prayers, or use the ones I've included.

CANDLE INTENTIONS

TO MAKE NEW FRIENDS

Candle color: Red

Day: Sunday

Crystal: Turquoise

Affirmation: "The universe brings me new and true friends. I draw positive, kind, and loving people to me."

TO STOP GOSSIP

Candle color: Orange

Day: Monday

Crystal: Black tourmaline

Affirmation: "My world is full of peace and harmony. There is no gossip, lies, or manipulation around me. I will not allow negative thoughts or conversation near me."

TO ATTRACT LOVE TO YOU

Candle color: Pink

Day: Begin your prayer on Tuesday if you're a girl. A guy starts on Friday.

Crystal: Rose quartz

Affirmation: "I draw perfect love to me. I am filled with the power of love and attraction. Perfect love is coming into my life."

TO BRING BACK A BOYFRIEND OR GIRLFRIEND

Candle color: Deep purple

Day: Friday

Crystal: Rose quartz, pink tourmaline

Affirmation: "Our relationship is healed and whole and _____ and I are working out all of our issues for our highest good."

TO PASS A TEST

Candle color: Yellow

Day: Wednesday

Crystal: Carnelian

Affirmation: "My mind is strong and clear. I am calm and relaxed as I take my test. I pass it with flying colors!"

TO INCREASE YOUR PSYCHIC ABILITY

Candle color: White

Day: Monday

Crystal: Amethyst

Affirmation: "I am open to receiving all of the wonderful gifts the universe has to offer me. My intuitive abilities are strong and expanding."

FOR PEACE IN THE FAMILY

Candle color: White

Day: Thursday

Crystal: Jade

Affirmation: "All is calm in our family. We are growing in love and light, peace, and harmony each day. The white light of protection surrounds my family."

FOR A NEW JOB

Candle color: Gold

Day: Sunday

Crystal: Citrine

Affirmation: "I give thanks for the wonderful and fulfilling work that is coming my way. I am able to prosper and grow because of this new opportunity."

TO WIN A CONTEST

Candle color: Green

Day: Friday

Crystal: Citrine

Affirmation: "I am lucky and fortunate. Good things come my way."

TO MAKE MORE MONEY

Candle color: Green

Day: Friday

Crystal: Citrine

Affirmation: "Prosperity and financial opportunities come my way. I am open to the
abundance of the universe."

TO GAIN MORE FULFILLMENT IN YOUR EVERYDAY LIFE

Candle color: Orange

Day: Sunday

Crystal: Emerald

Affirmation: "I feel whole and complete. My life is perfect. Each and
every day I am blessed."

TO DISPEL A NEGATIVE SITUATION

Candle color: White

Day: Monday

Crystal: Black tourmaline

Affirmation: "I am safe and protected. Any negative energies or situations are fading away as I speak. There is peace and harmony
all around me."

TO KEEP A LOVED ONE SAFE

Candle color: Silver

Day: Monday

Crystal: Clear quartz

Affirmation: "_____ is happy and safe and sound. No harm comes to [him/her]. _____ is protected and blessed."

FOR SAFE AND HAPPY TRIPS/TRAVEL

Candle color: Blue

Day: Thursday

Crystal: Garnet

Affirmation: "I am safe, secure, and happy wherever my travels may take me. I return home safely and refreshed from my trip."

FOR A NEW CAR

Candle color: Green

Day: Friday

Crystal: Citrine

Affirmation: "I will find the perfect, affordable vehicle for me. I give thanks for my new car."

TO LOSE WEIGHT

Candle color: Yellow

Day: Tuesday

Crystal: Sodalite

Affirmation: "I am losing weight in a healthy way. My body is feeling stronger each day. I am pleased and happy with the appropriate weight for my height and age."

TO OVERCOME AN ADDICTION

Candle color: Yellow

Day: Tuesday

Crystal: Onyx

Affirmation: "I am strong in my convictions and free from any addictions. My willpower is very strong and I can conquer any negative desires."

TO KEEP SOMEONE AWAY OR FROM BOTHERING YOU

Candle color: Silver

Day: Sunday

Crystal: Quartz

Affirmation: "I am free from negative people and situations. They cannot harm me or cause me any strife or worry."

TO DISPEL ANGER

Candle color: Blue

Day: Thursday

Crystal: Pearl

Affirmation: "I immediately release any anger, frustration, and hatred toward _____ regarding my present situation. I am at peace with the universe."

TO FORGIVE SOMEONE

Candle color: Blue

Day: Thursday

Crystal: Chrysocolla

Affirmation: "I forgive _____ for the harm, pain, hurt, and injustice [he/she] brought on me. I let go of any resentment [he/she] has caused me."

TO FEEL INNER PEACE

Candle color: White

Day: Monday

Crystal: Peridot

Affirmation: "I am calm and at one with the universe. I am filled with peace and happiness. My soul is fulfilled. Serenity and peace surround me."

FOR SPIRITUAL GROWTH AND DEVELOPMENT

Candle color: Blue

Day: Thursday

Crystal: Amethyst

Affirmation: "I am open to receive all of the spiritual gifts the universe wishes to send me. I am growing and developing on a deeper, spiritual path filled with higher knowledge and many blessings."

TO BUILD SELF-CONFIDENCE AND SELF-ESTEEM

Candle color: Red

Day: Sunday

Crystal: Citrine

Affirmation: "My self-confidence is growing. I know I am a wonderful, talented, bright, attractive person with so much to offer. I am proud of who I am and know I can conquer anything I set out to do. I am very powerful."

TO OVERCOME FEAR

Candle color: Gold

Day: Sunday

Crystal: Onyx

Affirmation: "I am free of any fear or anxiety. I release any worries. I am strong and know that I can overcome any adversity in my path."

TO MAKE THE RIGHT DECISIONS

Candle color: Blue

Day: Thursday

Crystal: Calcite

Affirmation: "I give thanks for the answers and knowledge to make the correct decision now. I am open to receiving truth and support from the universe."

TO AID IN MEDITATION

Candle color: Purple

Day: Wednesday

Crystal: Lapis lazuli

Affirmation: "The power of my higher self connects with the positive energies of our universe. I am able to freely expand my subconscious and use spiritual knowledge for my highest good."

TO ATTAIN SUCCESS

Candle color: Green

Day: Friday

Crystal: Emerald

Affirmation: "The universe is granting my every wish. I am successful. My goal is achieved. I give thanks for the abundance and happiness I am receiving. Success is mine!"

TO CHANGE YOUR LUCK

Candle color: Green

Day: Friday

Crystal: Citrine

Affirmation: "I am lucky. I am fortunate. All good things come my way. Any negative energies leave me immediately and my path is open to success."

FOR PROTECTION AGAINST EVIL OR NEGATIVE PEOPLE

Candle color: Black

Day: Saturday

Crystal: Black tourmaline

Affirmation: "I am safe and protected by the white light. No evil can come near me. I am strong and pure, secure in my own power. No negativity can harm or hinder me."

TO OVERCOME AN ILLNESS OR SICKNESS

Candle color: Light blue

Day: Thursday

Crystal: Bloodstone

Affirmation: "I am fine. My body is free from any illness or harm. Nothing but health and happiness surround me."

TO OVERCOME A DIFFICULT SITUATION

Candle color: Blue

Day: Thursday

Crystal: Blue lace agate

Affirmation: "I give thanks that I am able to overcome any difficulties and challenges in a positive way. Problems and obstacles fall by the wayside. My path is clear and inviting. No harm comes to me."

TO LEARN THE TRUTH ABOUT A MATTER

Candle color: White

Day: Monday

Crystal: Opal

Affirmation: "I can clearly see through my eyes, correctly hear through my ears, and understand the truth through my mind. No one can fool me. The truth has set me free!"

TO BETTER UNDERSTAND YOUR DREAMS

Candle color: White

Day: Monday

Crystal: Smoky quartz

Affirmation: "I am open to receiving the messages my dreams want to bring me. I clearly recall the details of my dreams when I awake each morning, and am able to interpret them thoroughly."

TO STOP JEALOUSY

Candle color: Greenish yellow

Day: Sunday

Crystal: Quartz

Affirmation: "Gone are the negative people with their envy and jealousy. I am not affected any longer by people whose jealousy consumes them."

FOR THE SOUL OF A DECEASED LOVED ONE

Candle color: White or gold

Day: Monday

Crystal: Rose quartz

Affirmation: "I pray for the soul of _____. I pray [his/her] soul is at peace and rest. I send [him/her] unending, everlasting love from my heart to [his/hers]!"

TO BE POPULAR

Candle color: Orange

Day: Tuesday

Crystal: Barite

Affirmation: "I am well liked and appreciated by my peers. They hold me in high regard, and recognize my talents and attributes in a positive and loving way."

WRITE YOUR OWN CANDLE
INTENTIONS HERE!

257

CHAPTER 8

SWEET DREAMS

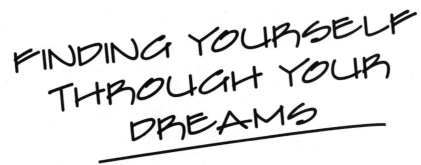

FINDING YOURSELF THROUGH YOUR DREAMS

Interpreting dreams can be a wonderful hobby. Think of them as your own private movie screening. Sometimes you play the leading role. Other times you're just an observer. These "movies" can be romantic, mysterious, action-oriented, scary, or just plain bizarre. If you dream a lot, you may be curious to find out what your dreams are trying to tell you. Understand the subconscious mind is trying to get your attention; perhaps there's important news coming, a riddle, or a story to unravel. Maybe there's a prediction of forthcoming events.

You can easily learn to interpret your dreams and even your nightmares. Dreaming is one way your subconscious mind can get you to listen. It has important things to tell you. Some people get psychic impressions through their dreams. Others may only dream when being forewarned about something. Some people say they never dream, but they do. They just can't remember.

We all dream. Sometimes we can recall our dreams vividly. Other times we wake up and can't remember a thing. Seldom do we know or understand the real significance of our dreams. A lot of them have hidden meanings. They could be prophetic in some way; give us a glimpse into our future. Some are so weird that they don't make any sense. You never know what or who you'll see in a dream.

Our friends and family members may make an appearance; even loved ones who have passed on. This next chapter will unlock some of the mysteries of your dreaming mind. Those born under the sign of Pisces dream a lot. Dreaming is how Pisces receive their psychic messages. However, all members of the zodiac can benefit from understanding dreams.

The first thing to bear in mind is there are two distinctly different types of dreams: prophetic and recurring. *Prophetic dreams* are those that can give us a glimpse into our future. They usually occur during the deepest part of our night's sleep, which is about 1 A.M. to 6 A.M. These are the dreams you will want to keep track of, record in a dream journal, and attempt to interpret.

Recurring dreams are dreams you have over and over again. The same theme is present. When I was younger, from about age seven to eighteen I had the same dream every so often. Burglars were breaking into my house and I was desperately trying to climb out of my bedroom window and run across the street to my neighbors. I felt safe there. Sometimes I awoke before I made it across the street, and other times I was able to reach my neighbor's back door before I woke up. I started keeping track of what was happening in my daily life every time I had this dream. I found the dream occurred when I was intimidated at school or anxious about something. For example, I'd have a difficult math test coming up and the dream would occur. I would be worried about an argument with a friend, go to bed, and the dream came up again. So, there I was, running away from something and looking for a safe haven. In my real life, I was just worried and trying to escape scary or intimidating situations. Now that I am older, I've only had this dream three times in the past twenty years.

If you are having recurring dreams, there usually is a psychological or emotional reason behind it. It's your subconscious mind's way of telling you that there is something you need to examine or look at within yourself.

There's another kind of dream too. It doesn't usually have any real significance, but you'll remember it vividly and with great detail. This would be the kind of dream you have when you've eaten too much pizza before going to bed! You've got the munchies at midnight, and then all night long your dreaming mind is in overdrive. Here's another scenario: You've just watched a scary movie. You're really into it, and then you immediately go to bed. Your mind hasn't relaxed or shut down, and similar images from the movie show up in your dream.

Let's look at the different categories that dreams fall into.

PRECOGNITIVE DREAMS

I call these *psychic dreams*. These are the ones you want to write down and take note of. They could come true! They will actually tell you what is coming up. Their detail may be a little off, but it's usually close.

My friend Mona had a dream that I was in Italy and was being followed in and out of stores by a handsome young Italian man. She saw me going into a bookstore, and this man kept watching and following close behind me. She said she didn't feel good about this guy and that he was kind of creepy. I was all alone. It was during the day, and I was indeed in Italy.

Well, several weeks later, my friend Julie asked me to go to Italy with her so she wouldn't have to travel alone on a business trip. I was very excited. By this time I had completely forgotten about my friend's dream. While Julie was tied up in meetings, I walked around Milan all by myself. I went into a huge department store and shopped in the stationary and book section. I noticed an older Italian man staring at me. I felt uncomfortable, and went into the children's department across the aisle. He followed me there, just glaring at me. I casually walked into another department—he followed. Then I got on the escalator and went downstairs. He got on the escalator too. Off I scurried into the perfume department. He was there! I made a beeline for the front door of the store through a crowd of people, hopped on the subway, and lost him. My friend's dream was right! But her description of this "stalker" was a little off. He wasn't handsome at all!

This is a good example of a prophetic dream. If one of your friends dreams about you, ask him or her for details. It could be nothing. It could be something silly. It could be important. Ask! It's best to remember details early in the day. You remember more right after you wake up and for the next few hours. As the day wears on, it's likely you'll lose a lot of the information or specific details in your dream. Try to write down as much as you can remember as soon as you wake up.

WARNING DREAMS

Depending on how you feel when you wake up, warning dreams can foretell of danger or problems ahead. Dreams such as this give us prior knowledge to change things or at least be aware. Many times we can avoid accidents or crisis if we are given significant warning. Unfortunately, most people don't take heed. They dismiss their dream as the result of an overactive imagination. But you really should listen. Your subconscious mind is trying tell you something.

I have a friend Char who one Sunday dreamed of a school that had yellow police tape all around it, the kind you see at crime scenes. She said it worried her because it seemed so real. There were little kids running out of the building and dozens of police cars parked at this school. She was frustrated because she didn't know exactly where the school was located. She felt helpless without more information. She wanted to be able to warn someone, but didn't know who. About two days later and twenty miles from where Char lives, a first-grader shot another classmate. The little girl died. The tragedy made national news for days. The events that occurred had unfolded in Char's warning dream. It could be considered a prophetic dream too.

There are other people I have counseled as an astrologer who have warning dreams and have been able to stop tragedy before it happens. One man from Michigan saw a motorcycle accident in his dream. He was driving the bike involved in the crash. He woke up sweating! He went out to the garage and started his Harley, trying to convince himself there was nothing to be afraid of. As he pulled out of the driveway, a speeding car barely missed him! That morning he placed an ad in the newspaper to sell his bike. He feels he was given a premonition and was able to avoid this accident, but wanted nothing more to do with any motorcycles.

FACTUAL DREAMS

We probably have more factual dreams than any other type of dream. They don't seem to last very long, and we get bits and pieces of information through these. Factual dreams are things we already know about. You could dream of taking a science test that you took yesterday, or of shopping for a new outfit for a dance. You could dream of having a conversation with a friend about something that is actually going on in your personal life.

I often dream I am giving clients readings. I give consultations almost every day, so I guess I do it in my sleep too. I recall in one dream giving a lady a very lengthy and detailed reading. I was mentally tired when I awoke, and felt like I had just completed a two-hour consultation. I probably had!

INSPIRATION DREAMS

If you are going through a personal problem with a friend, if you are having a difficult time at school or worrying about a project, an inspiration dream will offer a solution. It will give you an idea on how best to handle the situation. These dreams usually make you feel good. You'll get some answers. Again, remember to write the answers or solutions down right away so you don't forget them.

Here's another idea to help you when you're in the middle of a dilemma: if there's a decision you must make, but can't seem to find the right answer, ask yourself the question before you fall asleep at night. Let that be the last thing on your mind as you drift off. During your sleeping hours, your brain has time to process the question or dilemma without battling your emotional side. Your subconscious won't battle your conscious mind. In the morning, you will awake with the right answer. Don't question it! The first thing that comes to mind the next morning is the right answer! It works!

VISITATION DREAMS

I would like to address another type of dream: the visitation. Sometimes deceased loved ones come to us in a dream. They are likely around us during the day too. Their energy or presence is with us, but we cannot see or even feel them because our minds are cluttered. When we are asleep, our subconscious is more open to receiving their energy and the messages they want to bring us. This is one of the best times for our loved ones to contact us or make a spiritual connection. Let's distinguish between a simple dream of a loved one and an actual visitation.

A dream is something you will remember when you first awaken in the morning. It will fade over the next few hours and days, and then eventually you may have no memory of it at all. A visitation is an actual visit from the soul or spirit of someone. It feels like a dream, but you will remember it vividly. It will stay with you all day, for weeks and months and perhaps even years later.

My father passed on a few years ago. I missed him desperately. Through my dreams I knew I could connect with him. It was such a wonderful feeling! Actually, a few years before he died, I said, "Daddy, if you ever die, please come to me in a dream. I won't be scared. Please promise me you will." He kept this promise.

Initially after someone passes on, his or her spirit may still linger with family and friends who are grieving. My dad knew I needed him, and this was the only way he could reach me. He came to me many times during my sleep over a course of two years. I wrote down everything about these dreams.

There was one particular dream I absolutely knew was a visitation. My father's spirit had come to visit me. I was still having a hard time with his passing. We were standing in our kitchen and he hugged me. I felt him hug me and tell me everything would be all right.

I came out of the dream with such a blessed and joyful feeling! It was wonderful.

My dad came other times and talked with me about some of the difficulties I was going through and assured me everything would be all right. He doesn't come as much as he used to, but it seems when I ask him and really need to reconnect with him, he will show up in a dream. I consider these dreams a special time I can spend with my dad. It really is time we spend together.

If there is someone you miss, know that you can still connect with that person. Ask him or her to come to you. You should not use this opportunity just for fun or to test the theory, but use it for when you really need that loved one. Many times dearly departed family and friends will come to us to offer support when we are in a crisis.

INTERPRETING YOUR DREAMS

Like anything else, the more you practice, the more you will understand and be able to interpret the meaning of your dreams. I suggest keeping a dream journal and getting a good, thick dream interpretation book. Don't invest in one that has a few descriptions with little information in it. Get a large one that goes into great detail.

Generally, you are the best interpreter of your dreams. Your subconscious mind will give you answers. But if you are having trouble deciphering meanings, you can always see a reputable dream analyst. A dream interpreter is someone who has studied the meaning of dreams—both the psychological and spiritual meanings—and can explain what your dream is trying to tell you.

Did you know that even a bizarre or bad dream may actually have a good omen? Just because you have a scary dream doesn't always mean it is a bad one. This is another reason to have a detailed dream guide next to your bed!

What happens when two people share the same dream? Let's go back to my dreaming friend, Mona. Mona has a neighbor who is in a wheelchair. She had a dream one night that this neighbor was able to walk. In her dream, Mona told the neighbor, "Let me help you up. Let's see if you can walk." Back to reality now: the next day, this neighbor called Mona and proceeded to tell her about her own dream. She said Mona was helping her out of the wheelchair and she began walking across the floor! Mona couldn't believe her ears! Hopefully this is a precognitive dream too. The fact that both women had the same dream the same night meant they both were given the same information. Details varied, but for the most part, the dream was the same. Now, for the interesting part: Mona's neighbor recently had an operation and has regained feeling in her legs!

I find that when two people have the same dream, it is usually a prophetic one, and one person is to share or help the other person through something. The information is so important that by both people dreaming the same dream, it will not be dismissed or go unnoticed. These types of dreams should be taken seriously and could possibly come true. By all means, interpret these dreams down to the last detail.

THE DREAM JOURNAL

You can buy dream journals in almost any bookstore, or you can make your own. They can be very simple. Just a spiral notebook will work. Keep the journal next to your bed along with a pen or pencil. You can also leave a tape recorder on your nightstand, so when you wake up you can record what you remember.

Date the journal and begin writing anything and everything you can remember. You can write it in sequence or bits and pieces. Remember the colors, numbers, faces, places, people, discussions, times, and season of the year. Specific details are important. Throughout the day, if you recall anything else, write it down and add it to your journal later if you need to. No information is insignificant, but some is more important than other.

Dreams are made up of many elements. There is usually a main theme in every dream. Pick the one thing that stands out in your mind as being the most vivid or important. Analyze or begin to interpret that first. Remember, you are the best interpreter of your own dreams.

Ask first what does it mean to you? Then look up the individual meanings in your dream book. If your dream is full of detail, this means it is very important. If you only remember small bits and pieces and it fades quickly, I wouldn't write much, if anything, in your journal. It may not have any meaning unless it is linked to another dream you've had in the past.

HERE'S AN EXAMPLE
DREAM JOURNAL PAGE!

Date _____

1. Describe the dream.

2. How do you feel about the dream? (Happy, upset, confused?)

3. What was the main theme or element of the dream?

4. What were the minor details in your dream?

5. Were there any special people, places, colors, or numbers in your dream?

6. Was there a specific time frame involved? (Current, future, or past?)

7. Does this dream seem familiar? Did you experience this dream before?

8. Read your dream book and write the interpretation here.

9. With all of the information listed above, what do you think this dream means?

Accident: If you dream of an accident, it is usually meant as a warning. Try to avoid unnecessary travel for a few weeks. Don't drive carelessly. If you can remember what or who was involved in the accident, try to avoid that thing or person for at least the next few days.

Achievement: You will reach a goal and feel very proud of yourself. If you're working on a special project and wonder how it will turn out, this dream is telling you you will be successful!

Acne: There will be disappointment in a love affair, but better relationships are around the bend.

Afraid: To dream of being afraid is often not as bad as it seems. It actually means you will overcome any difficulties in the next few weeks.

Alien: Ever dream of a man from outer space? It means you will make new friends and many important changes in your life.

Angel: Protection and happiness are coming your way!

Animals: Animals can be good omens, but it really depends on how they appear to you in your dream. If they were friendly, you will have a great week or two! If they were angered or vicious, you may experience disappointments instead.

Athletics: If you play sports, this is not a particularly big deal. But if you don't, this dream means you will have some tense moments. Expect a doctor or dentist appointment in the near future.

Baby: This dream can have many different meanings, depending on what the baby looked like. If it was pretty, the dream means your friends will be loyal and help you if needed. If the baby was ugly, watch out for someone in your social circle who is two-faced.

Barefoot: If you're entirely naked in your dream, you will be very lucky. If only your feet were bare, then expect some troubling times.

Basement: A basement means don't bow to peer pressure. Stand strong in your beliefs. You could be influenced by friends to do things you shouldn't.

Beasts: A lot of kids dream of scary monsters. They represent problems and delays ahead. However, if you managed to scare the beasts away, the dream means you will overcome any difficulties in your path.

Book: You will have a pleasant, peaceful life.

Boys: This is a good omen. Lucky times are coming!

Brother: If you're a girl, dreaming of your brother means family harmony. If you're a guy, this dream foretells family fights.

Bugs: Usually this dream gives you a warning that some of your friends could be negative.

Bus: If you're riding a bus, this dream means you are making progress.

Butterfly: You will be popular and well liked.

Cake: Any kind of dream involving a cake is considered lucky!

Calendar: Your worries are coming to an end.

Chocolate: To dream of chocolate candy means your health will be good.

Christmas: If you dream of this holiday in any month other than December, there will be happy times ahead.

Climbing: You will succeed at whatever you are doing.

Clown: You should seriously think about changing your friends.

Coins: There will be unexpected money coming your way!

Colors: The interpretation of this dream is based on the particular color in it. The colors have different meanings.

Blue: Means you will have peace and harmony.

Pink: Means great success in your love life.

Green: Expect a nice trip or vacation.

Purple: There will be a short period of unhappiness. It will not last.

Yellow: If you're working hard to accomplish something, expect some setbacks, but you will have success.

Black: Bad omen. There could be danger or unlucky times ahead.

Brown: You'll have more money soon!

Red: Good news is coming.

Concert: If you were attending a concert, unexpected good news will come your way.

Cookies: Beware of little arguments over nothing with friends and family.

Costume: *See* Disguise.

Dance: There's a new love on the horizon.

Danger: This is a dream that actually means the reverse. You will overcome any difficulties that lie ahead.

Digging: This means harder work is coming up, or you need to buckle down to your studies.

Disguise: If you saw yourself in some sort of costume or disguise, it means you will be part of a devious scheme and be embarrassed.

Dog: Dogs are usually a good omen. But if you see them fighting, it may mean you and a friend of yours have quarrels of your own.

Door: A closed door means you have missed some opportunities. An open door means your hopes, wishes, and dreams will come true.

Eagle: An eagle flying means a good job is ahead.

Earrings: In a girl's dream, this is a warning to stay away from gossip.

Elevator: If you are going up, this is good. Circumstances are looking up for you. If the elevator is going down, it means you are on your way down!

Escape: This dream can be interpreted only by looking at details.
From an angry animal: You will find that you have untrustworthy friends.
From a fire: You will succeed, even though you are worried.
From being held prisoner: You will gain popularity quickly.

If you couldn't escape in your dream: You may be going through a hard time, and it will take a while for things to work out.

Eyes: Usually a good omen of pleasant news to come.
Scary eyes: Someone is going to deceive you.
Animal or beast-like eyes: There is hidden jealousy around you.
Brown eyes: A new love is on the horizon.
Blue eyes: A new friendship is coming.

Fairy: You will get your heart's desire when you least expect it.

Falling: This is one of the most common dreams, but it has many meanings. Usually it means there is some sort of fear that you are holding on to. This fear is holding you back from expanding your life.

Fame: To dream of being famous means that you are trying to reach a goal that is unrealistic.

Family: Things will turn around in your favor. You will get your way!

Farewell: Saying goodbye means there will be a break-up in a current relationship.

Fear: *See* Afraid.

Feathers: You will have a stroke of luck, popularity, and happiness.

Fish: If you saw fish swimming, it means money will be coming to you. Dead fish mean sorrow and disappointments.

Flies: Your friends are jealous of you.

Flowers: You will find lots of things to be happy about. Dead flowers is a warning not to be careless.

Flying: You have great ambition and will reach your goal.

Friends: This is a good omen of happy times ahead.

Future: If you dream of your future, it means there are many unexpected changes coming into your life.

Gate: If the gate is closed, there will be an obstacle in your path you must overcome. If it is open, you have the go-ahead with a new idea or plan. A locked gate means major obstacles.

Ghost: This dream is warning you not to participate in some upcoming scheme or activity. Resist temptation or pressure from other people.

Girl: To dream of a girl means there is some sudden, surprising news.

Gossip: Don't tell anyone your deepest secrets. They will be found out!

Grandparents: They represent security and protection for you.

Gum: If you were chewing gum, don't trust everyone.

Hallway: A long hallway means a long period of worry. A grand hall indicates wonderful changes.

Handbag: If you lost it, this means you have problems coming your way. If you find a purse, you will overcome any difficulties. Sometimes this dream means more money is coming to you.

Hero: A new offer is coming with money. There could be a raise in your allowance or a new job.

History: New and sudden opportunities fall into your lap.

Horse: Riding horses means you are becoming more popular or moving up in the world.

House: An old house means you will be seeing friends from your past. A new house means more money.

Ice cream: Major success and advantages.

Idol: You will be told a secret. Do not breathe a word of it to anyone!

Jealousy: You will likely be involved in a series of problems regarding your love life and important friendships.

Journey: You will feel as if your whole world is changing.

Ketchup: A new friend of the opposite sex is coming into your life.

Kidnap: If you were kidnapped, you will soon be embarrassed about something. If you kidnapped someone, something could be stolen from you.

Kittens: For a girl, dreaming of kittens means a happy love affair, but it will not last. For a guy, there will be disappointment in his love life.

Leopard: You may have hidden enemies around you.

Lie: If you dreamed you told lies, you will have trouble because you are acting foolish.

Light: You will feel excited and hopeful about something you gave up on a while ago.

Love: Happiness.

Mansions: If the mansion was elegant, you may experience a change that you do not like. If it was empty, these changes will be to your liking.

Marriage: For single people to dream they are getting married means they are coming into a relationship that will not last and they should look elsewhere for love.

Mask: Deceit. People you associate with are not being honest.

Money: If you are receiving money in your dream, this is usually a good omen. Finding money means you will have mixed blessings. Losing money actually means a windfall is coming to you.

Monsters: *See* Beasts.

Mountain: Seeing a mountain in your dream is the classic obstacle dream. Simply put, there is something you must get over.

Naked: If you're entirely naked in your dream, you will be very lucky.

Ocean: A calm ocean means good times for you and your buddies. A stormy ocean means you will need courage to overcome problems in the next few weeks.

Parade: Expect more money to come your way.

Parents: If you dream of your dad, you will have good luck with work or a new job. If your mom shows up in a dream, expect a new boyfriend or girlfriend to come into your life.

Pimples. *See* Acne.

Pirate: The pirate dream tells you of exciting new ventures, but be cautious of new people. They may not be true friends.

Police: You have security. You are safe.

Purse: *See* Handbag.

Race: This is an obstacle dream. If you win the race, expect good things to come your way. If you lose, it means you have to work harder to accomplish your goals.

Rain: You'll see huge improvements in a current situation.

Rainbow: Say goodbye to your troubles. There will be great happiness.

Rats: You will have trouble because of jealous people. However, white rats mean you will be protected against negative people.

Rattlesnake: Someone around you is lying— possibly a new love interest.

Road: If the road in your dream is straight, you will have smooth, steady progress over the next few weeks. If it is bumpy or rough, know that you will have to overcome some problems.

Robber: You are in danger of losing your head in love.

Running: You would like to escape from something.

School: You may have a problem with money for a few days. It also means you need to let go of the past and be open to learning new things.

Sister: For a girl to dream of her sister, there may be family troubles ahead. For a guy, it means he will feel emotionally secure about himself.

Snake: The snake can warn of lots of troubles, accidents, and the danger of being cheated by someone.

Sports. *See* Athletics.

Stealing: Be more cautious with your money and how you spend it.

Teacher: To dream of a teacher means there will be arguments with parents or authority figures. This is not a good period to argue, and you should try to avoid getting grounded or punished over the next few weeks.

Teeth: Broken teeth mean a love affair is ending. Getting your teeth pulled means there is a good job coming soon. Loose teeth mean you may have some untrustworthy friends. Nice, white teeth mean you will have happiness.

Travel: To take a journey foretells of a change in your money or popularity.

Vampire: You could be experiencing a lot of emotional conflict.

Watch: Your friends will help you get ahead in life.

Zodiac: If you had a dream about the signs of the zodiac, you will one day have great success, fame, and fortune.

WRITE YOUR OWN DREAM
INTERPRETATIONS HERE!

_____
_____
_____
_____
_____
_____
_____
_____
_____
_____
_____
_____
_____
_____
_____
_____
_____

CHAPTER

9

KNOW IT ALL

DEVELOPING YOUR PSYCHIC POWERS

We are all psychic and sensitive beings. Everyone has intuitive powers, but some people have developed them and use these spiritual gifts more than others. There are other people who are scared of "seeing" things and deny these gifts. Intuition is certainly nothing to be frightened or intimidated by. The more you use it, the more it grows and becomes a natural part of your everyday existence.

What kind of pictures does the word *psychic* conjure up for you? An old Gypsy woman with a crystal ball? A wizard? Perhaps you think of Ms. Cleo on the psychic hot line.

Well, psychics, mediums, astrologers, and card readers come from all walks of life these days. No longer are they found in dimly lit rooms with flashing neon signs advertising their craft. Many are holistic health practitioners, nurses, psychologists, teachers, and people who have developed a gift and wish to share it. Many teach other people how to develop their own skills through workshops, books, and lectures. The New Age field is exploding and becoming more mainstream. Almost everyone has had their palm read or gotten a tarot reading these days.

Palmists, card readers, astrologers, and other New Age professionals are setting up private offices, hosting television and radio programs, and joining lecture circuits. All are using their psychic powers, but some use different tools to aid them in receiving messages and forecasting. Because there are so many different types of readings available, I've compiled a list of some of the most popular types of readings.

Astrology: The science of using planetary influences to read the past, present, and future.

Aura reading: Reading the colors in a person's energy field to determine one's personality.

Candle reading: Looking into the flames of a burning candle for visions.

Card reading: Using a regular deck of playing cards to read the past, present, and future.

Channeling: A psychic goes into a trance-like state and channels other energies or spirits to receive messages. The spirit works through the reader, who passes information on to you.

Clairaudience: The reader receives messages from spirits by listening.

Dream analysis: Interpreting dreams to determine messages from the subconscious.

Graphology: Handwriting analysis; the study of a person's writing to predict personality traits.

Numerology: The study of numbers in a person's name or birth date to predict events and life path.

Palmistry: The study of the lines of the palms.

Past-life regression: A regressionist guides you back to a previous life through the use of hypnotherapy or meditation. The goal is to see who and what you were in a previous lifetime to help solve issues, problems, or patterns in your current lifetime. You may also be able to discover with whom you have had a past-life connection.

Psychic: One who uses his intuition to make predictions. Sometimes psychics visualize or see events unfolding in their mind's eye.

Psychometry: The reader senses vibrations by holding personal items such as a ring or watch. Through the sense of touch, the reader will receive psychic impressions.

Scrying: Making predictions using a crystal ball or a plate to see images.

Seer: Also known as a psychic; a person who sees the past, present, and future through her mind's eye.

Tarot: A seventy-eight-card deck used to look at the past, present, and future.

Tea-leaf reading: Using the leaf formation and images found in a tea cup to predict upcoming events.

Since the early 1990s I have organized psychic fun fairs and expos around the country. I have hired readers of all types to work at these events. I am often asked "What is the best type of reading to get?" and "Where can I find a good psychic?" These are very important questions and they deserve detailed answers.

First of all, many readers will not give readings to young people under the age of eighteen without a parent's or guardian's permission. So it's a good idea to get your parent's okay before you book an appointment with a reader.

HOW DO YOU FIND A GOOD READER?

I suggest getting referrals. If you have friends or family members who have had their cards or palm read, ask them how they liked the reader and if their predictions proved accurate.

Looking in the phone book or calling a 900-line is risky and can be expensive. You can attend a psychic fair if they have them in your area and ask fair-goers for their opinions of the individual readers.

Here's a list of good rules to follow:

1. Ask around. Get referrals.

2. If you call for information, go with your gut feeling. How do you feel about the reader?

3. Never let anyone push you into booking an appointment with them.

4. Avoid 900-lines unless they have a good reputation and you can be connected to a specific psychic that comes recommended. Some psychics have their own extension lines. But the cost of 900-lines can add up, so be careful.

5. Don't assume the most expensive reader is the best. I have been to big-name readers who have charged several hundred dollars for a session and absolutely nothing they told me came true. Likewise, I've spent ten dollars at a fair and the psychic was right on the money.

6. Ask the reader what her fee is, and also about the specific type of reading you can expect: how long the session will last, what

you need to bring to the appointment, and if you are allowed to ask questions after the reading is finished.

7. Ask if you can bring a tape recorder or take notes. Some readers do not allow recordings of the sessions; others welcome it.

8. Don't be afraid to ask readers to tell you a little bit about their experience. For example, how long have they been reading and what do they specialize in? Some readers specialize in specific areas such as relationships and health.

WHEN YOU BOOK YOUR APPOINTMENT

1. Be on time. Come with an open mind. Don't be nervous. Many times, seeing a reader is just like going into a counseling session. There really isn't anything spooky about it. But first-timers can be a little intimidated, so relax. Take a few deep breaths.

2. Sit directly in front of the reader unless you are directed to do otherwise. Don't cross your arms or legs, as this can block energy between you and the psychic.

3. Don't start talking and asking a lot of questions upfront. Let the reader do the talking. See what she or he has to say first. If you are telling the reader everything about yourself, then you are not getting a reading. The psychic can be influenced by what you are saying and this may influence the outcome of your reading. I like to do what I call a "cold read" first. I prefer to begin without the client asking any questions, thus allowing me to see what I "pick up." Then I ask for questions toward the end of the session.

4. If a reader is asking you for a lot of information, then you are not getting your money's worth. You are giving the reader information to build on. There is a difference between this and confirming if the reader is on the right track. For example, a good reader will not ask, "How old are you? Do you have a boyfriend? Are you in school? What hobbies you do have?" The reader should be telling you these things!

Sometimes a reader will ask you for confirmation to make sure she is on the right track. For example: "I see you are working part-time right now on the weekends at a restaurant. Is this correct?" Then this is okay to answer back. It helps the reader to know she is on the right track and then can move on to further predictions.

It is not polite to shake your head no all of the time, even if the reader is telling you things that you do not agree with or understand at the time. Perhaps he is telling you of things that will happen in the future. Be open to the information, write it down, and see what manifests in the future. After all, you are here to see what lies ahead!

5. Have a list of questions. After the reader is finished, he may ask you if you have any questions. Some he may have already answered, but if not, here's your chance. You can ask now for more details and clarification about something that was already discussed in the reading.

OTHER INFORMATION

If you find a good medium, hang on to him. There are a lot of ordinary readers out there, but there are very few that are great! Remember, no one is 100 percent accurate, but you should expect a reader to be at least 80 to 85 percent accurate on making predictions. Finding a reader who "clicks" with you is important too.

Your best friend may see a psychic that she rants and raves about. That psychic may be 90 percent accurate on your friend's predictions, but just so-so for you. Shopping for a reader is like shopping for a good pair of shoes. Some fit just right, and others don't!

There are some psychics who will make a personal connection right away with you, and others whom you will walk away from wondering "What did she really tell me?" Have a little patience and an open mind and don't give up. Besides referrals, you can find psychics at New Age fairs, expos, and on the Internet.

Don't waste a lot of money trying out different people. You can get mini-readings at fairs for as little as ten dollars. The average reading, depending on the area in which you live, can range from thirty to ninety dollars. In larger cities, and with psychics who have appeared on television and radio, fees may be higher—ranging from one hundred to six hundred dollars.

Some people try to "test" the reader. They'll ask, "Tell me, what did I have for breakfast today?" or "What is my mom's name?" While there are some psychics who may be able to answer these questions, you can't reasonably expect a psychic to know everything. A medium receives messages, but not always the ones you expect to hear.

WHAT YOU SHOULD EXPECT FROM A READING

1. An average full reading can last anywhere from twenty minutes to an hour. Some readers can give you quite a bit of information in as little as twenty minutes. If you have a lot of issues, you may need more time, so an hour is not unreasonable—especially for an in-depth astrology reading.

2. Your reader should give you details and possible time frames for events to unfold.

3. Beside personality traits and reading the past, a reader should be able to give you predictions for your future. Some readings are good for three to six months, and others are good for up to a year. Ask your reader how long your reading is good for.

4. The reader should allow you to ask a few questions.

On another note, I want you to know that nothing is written stone. If you do not like something in your reading, you can change it. We get readings to tell us of times of opportunity and to warn us when to be cautious. If I were to read your cards and say, "Be careful, you could get a speeding ticket tomorrow on I-75 and 11 Mile Road," you can change the outcome of what could happen. You either won't drive that road tomorrow, or you'll be extra cautious. So remember, you can change what is said. You do have control over your own destiny.

I do not believe psychics should tell people anything bad unless they have a chance to change it. This is one reason first-timers are scared to get a reading—because they don't want to hear anything bad. I have heard horror stories of psychics telling people they have a dark cloud over their head or a hex is on them. Then the so-called psychic wanted the client to pay four hundred dollars to burn candles to take the spell away. These are the type of readers who give the truly gifted and spiritual readers a bad name. These bad apples have caused our New Age industry to be looked down upon or with skepticism.

Scam artists as such prey on people's emotions and make empty promises. They do exist and there are plenty of them out there. If you encounter such a scam artist, refuse to believe and immediately leave. Do not give them any of your money. I also suggest turning them into the local law enforcement agency. This is another reason why referrals are the way to go when searching for a reader.

A good, honest reader will give you choices. He will give you encouragement, options, and be positive and upbeat. You should feel happy and full of hope and direction after a reading, not frightened. If there is a challenging period approaching, a good reader will tell you how to work around it, deal with it, or completely avoid it. You are the only person who controls your own destiny. A reading is like a flashlight: it can light up your path and show you things, but you can choose to walk it or not.

DEVELOPING YOUR PSYCHIC POWERS

Throughout this book, you've learned a lot about the different New Age arts. One thing we haven't covered yet is how you can develop your own intuitive abilities and psychic powers.

One of the best ways for beginners to get started is to learn to meditate. You need to clear your mind of any outside thoughts, and be quiet and still, inside and out. This takes practice. It can take weeks and months to be able to achieve this state of relaxation. If your mind is cluttered and busy, your subconscious mind cannot work through all of the mess to deliver messages.

PREPARE TO MEDITATE

When you first begin to meditate, you should find a private place in your home where you will not be disturbed. It should be a sacred space. There should be no televisions or radio or computers in that corner, and you should use it only for meditation. Keep this area clean and clutter-free. Turn off your telephones and answering machines and make sure no one will disturb or interrupt you. If you like, you can have a little shrine or altar in this space. Always take a bath or shower before you meditate so you are clean. Some people burn incense or candles. Others put crystals and flowers in their sacred space.

POSTURE

It is important that you find a comfortable and proper position to meditate in. Most people sit upright with their spine straight and erect. You don't want your body to be stiff; it should be relaxed. You should always be comfortable. If you have a comfy chair, use it. Sometimes you may want to sit in what is known as the lotus position. Some people have pillows they use for meditation or a small three-legged meditation stool. Remember, I want you to feel comfortable, so use what works for you.

You really shouldn't meditate while lying down because it's easy to doze off and fall into a deep sleep. Your breathing isn't as controlled either. Breathing is one of the most important tools to create a positive meditation.

BREATHING

During a meditation, it is important you concentrate on your breath. The first thing you should do is take a deep, slow breath. Then slowly exhale. Do this several times. Do not try to hold your breath. Never do anything that makes you feel dizzy or uncomfortable during your meditation. If you get a headache, then stop and try to meditate later in the day. As you inhale, visualize yourself inhaling a beautiful white light, a light of peace. Feel as if with every breath you take in you are breathing in joy, peace, and harmony. As you exhale, breathe out any anxiousness, anger, or hurt you have felt earlier in the day or are hanging on to. As you breathe in, know that you are taking in cosmic energy.

EYES CLOSED?

You have probably seen pictures of people meditating with their eyes closed. Most people will fall asleep if they keep their eyes closed during a meditation. I suggest you keep your eyes half open. Perhaps focus your eyes on a pleasing object in your sacred space such as a flower or a photo.

PREPARING AND FOCUSING YOUR MIND

The most important part of meditation is to clear your mind. This is also the hardest thing to do. But once you learn to do it, it becomes second nature. You need to calm and empty your mind. Think of nothing, even if it's only for a few moments. Then increase the time a few minutes, then ten or fifteen minutes. If it helps, visualize an empty TV screen. See nothing; expect nothing. Concentrate on this empty screen.

When you feel you have achieved a relaxed or divine state of being, ask your mind some questions. Better yet, see what comes in—what thoughts or messages come. Ask your angel or spirit guide to channel messages to you. If there is anything that doesn't seem right to you, or if you feel negative energy around you, immediately put the white light around your body and refuse to process or validate that thought. Think of only divine, good, and pure thoughts.  When you're ready to come out of the meditation, come out slowly and gradually become more aware of your breathing. Slowly return to a more conscious state. You may want to write down some of the messages and thoughts that came to you in the meditation.

By learning to meditate, you're opening your higher self to receive messages. Your psychic abilities will grow, and you will be able to receive a clear channel when you give readings or use your intuitive abilities to help yourself and others. Meditation can also help relax you and take stress away.

Meditation is a good tool, but there are also other tools to use to expand your psychic abilities. We talked about some of the them in other chapters. Below are a few exercises you can do to open your intuitive mind. The more you do these exercises, the more your abilities will develop and grow.

MIND-READING DEVELOPMENT EXERCISE

Have a friend sit face-to-face with you. Place your hand on his to feel his energy. Ask him to think of a color. When you first try this technique, you may want to limit the choices. For example, you can tell him to pick from three colors like red, pink, and blue. Have him choose a color in his mind, but do not have

him tell you his choice. Tell your friend to visualize and think of that color until you tell him to stop. Concentrate, clear your mind, and "feel" what color he has chosen. Silently ask yourself, "What is the color he is thinking of at this very moment?" Choose the very first color that comes to your mind. Don't second-guess your first thought. If you were concentrating correctly, you'll be right on the money. Continue to use this exercise to test your accuracy rate. Increase the number of colors to choose from as your accuracy rate grows.

Eight out of ten right answers are great! Six out of ten aren't bad. If you only get two right, don't be discouraged. You may just need to learn to concentrate more. Go back and work on the meditation and mind-clearing techniques. Try again later!

VISUALIZATION

STEP ONE: VISUALIZING THE PAST

Close your eyes, relax your body, your mind, and visualize something that has already happened; something you know to be true. For example, see yourself on a recent shopping trip with your friend. Visualize a store you visited. Take your time and see all of the details, just like you saw them that day. What did you buy? How much was it? See the sales clerk. See any detail you can remember. Put them in sequence. What you are doing is using a technique called *visualization*. You can "go back" to that time and place.

Your mind will recall what happened. Remembering and being able to "see" the past helps you develop and strengthen your skills to see the future. Once you have accomplished this, let's move on to the next step: visualizing the present.

STEP TWO: VISUALIZING THE PRESENT

Close your eyes and visualize someone or a situation you know to be true; something that is occurring right now. Are you home? Are you in your room? Is your mom cooking dinner? Whatever you know for a fact to be happening at this very moment, visualize it. See the details in your mind's eye. This is the easiest of all three steps to do, but take your time. Slow down, see everything around you. Your goal is to get "lost in the moment," the exact moment. Do not think any further ahead than right now. Take a few minutes to do this. Be very aware of your senses and feelings now. Once you've spent several minutes refining this technique, you can move on to seeing your future!

STEP THREE: VISUALIZING THE FUTURE

By visualizing the past and present, you are exercising your mind to become more open to see things. It's easy to think of the past and the present. Logically, you know that as your reality. Now, let's take the *big* step in developing your psychic abilities. Let's visualize your future!

Clear your mind as you learned in meditation. Pick a subject: school, your job, hanging out with your best friend. Imagine yourself there. Now, concentrate on how this specific time will be spent. How do you feel? Visualize the setting, the place. See the people around you. You can even ask your mind a question, such as, "What is going to happen tomorrow at school?" Allow your mind to answer you. Sometimes the answer will come even before you finish your question. If this happens, your psychic abilities are turned on! If it doesn't, ask yourself the question and wait for the answer. It will come. Don't second-guess any information that comes through. Even if it seems silly, write it down and don't dismiss it. Then tomorrow, see the events unfold. Sometimes they will unfold exactly as you saw them, and other times there will be subtle messages, depending on how you interpreted the information. This technique works, but it may take time, practice, and patience on your part to develop it. Use your notes to confirm or validate what happens.

TELEPATHY

"Tele-" reminds me of *television* and *telephone,* a form of communication, sending messages across the lines; "-pathy" reminds me of a *path.* To me, telepathy is sending and receiving specific messages through a line of energy to a specific path, destination, or person. You can use your mind like a telephone line, or turn it on like a TV set and send out your signals.

Let's say you send a loving thought to your boyfriend or girlfriend right now. Your thoughts are like energy. This vibration is sent out into the universe and locates its target. Your true love will feel this thought and think of you. If you concentrate real hard, your phone will start ringing and it'll be your boyfriend or girlfriend on the line! How many times have you thought about someone and that person calls a few moments later? Telepathy is becoming more aware of the messages sent out by others, and being able to send them out into the universe.

One of the best ways to increase and test your psychic power is to give a reading to someone you don't know very well. Don't be intimidated; just do it. Ask one of your friends to introduce you to someone new. Sit across from your new acquaintance and just tell him the first things that come into your mind about his personality, his life, and any other ideas that may form. Just let it happen. Let your thoughts flow. At this point, don't concentrate on being "right." Just see what comes. Then ask for confirmation when things do arise. Check with your "client" a few months down the road to see if your predictions were accurate.

THE MOST IMPORTANT LESSON OF ALL

Trusting your inner voice is the most important thing I can tell you. You can work with all of the wonderful tools laid out before you in this book, but unless you trust yourself, your opinion, your first thought, then you are not developing your psychic potential.

Always listen to the first thought or impression that comes into your mind. If your stomach is upset, if your body reacts to a situation or a person in a certain way, if you feel positive or negative about something, go with it. Your body won't lie. Your senses won't deceive you.

Your abilities are there, ready to be used and developed. You have these special powers just waiting to be put to use. Use them for your highest good and those of others. If you ever use your abilities to manipulate, hurt, or control someone, negative responses will come back to you. Just like a boomerang, whatever you put out will return to you.

Cherish these abilities. Use them not for fun or games, but to create and manifest a most wondrous life for yourself. Your dreams will come true. Don't believe it when you see it, believe it and then you will see it! Know in your heart that by using the special powers and tools at your disposal, anything in life is possible. Go after your heart's desire.

Expect good to come to you. Throw out any negative thoughts. Replace them with your higher power. May love and light surround you on your spiritual journey!

GLOSSARY

Astrology: The study of the influence of the planets and stars.

Aura: Color and energy surrounding the body.

Aura photograph: A picture of a person and his or her aura.

Channeling: To bring forth messages by connecting with another spirit.

Children lines: The lines in the palm that predict how many children one will have.

Crystal: Three-dimensional structure made up of atoms, molecules, and ions with individual healing properties and specific energies.

Decan: A period that each zodiac sign is divided into that is equal to about ten days of a birth month. For example, April 20–29 is considered the first decan of Taurus.

Dream journal: A notebook used to record your dreams.

Fate line: The line in the palm that tells of your karma and destiny.

Gemstone: A precious or semiprecious stone that has been cut and polished.

Graphology: The study of handwriting for the purpose of analyzing character and personality.

Head line: The line in the palm that characterizes the logic, reason, and intellect of a person.

Heart line: The line in the palm that characterizes the emotions and love life of a person.

Intuition: Knowing and sensing things without using a rational process.

Karma: The total effect of one's actions; destiny.

Life line: The line in the palm that foretells the health and sometimes longevity of a person.

Lotus position: A position used for meditation purposes. See illustration on page 293.

Major arcana: Twenty-two out of the seventy-eight cards in a tarot deck. These are said to hold the Greater Secrets.

Marriage lines: The lines in the palm that suggest marriage.

Meditate: To think deeply and quietly on a higher level of consciousness.

Minor arcana: Fifty-six cards of the seventy-eight cards in a tarot deck. These represent lesser secrets than the major arcana.

Numerology: The study of numbers and their influence on life.

Occult: Having to do with the supernatural.

Palmistry: The study of the lines in the palms to predict the future and basic personality traits.

Psychic: A sensitive and intuitive person who can feel, sense, and predict the future.

Psychometry: Sensing vibrations from personal objects such as rings and watches to predict the future.

Seer: A person who is able to visualize and predict the future.

Tarot: A set of fortunetelling cards.

Tea-leaf reading: The art of foretelling the future by looking at the remaining leaves in a tea cup.

Telepathy: Communication between individuals by using mental processes rather than ordinary sensory means.

Zodiac: A band in the celestial sphere divided into twelve astrological signs, each bearing the name of its constellation.

SUGGESTED READING

Buckland, Raymond. *Practical Candleburning Rituals.* St. Paul, Minn.: Llewellyn Publications, 1970.

Goodman, Linda. *Linda Goodman's Star Signs.* New York: St. Martin's Press, 1987.

Hewitt, William. *Astrology for Beginners.* St. Paul, Minn.: Llewellyn Publications, 1991.

Lake, Gina. *Pathways to Self-Discovery.* Willow Springs, Mo.: Nucleus Publications, 1994.

Morningstar, Sally, ed. *Divining the Future.* London: Hermes House, 2001.

Parker, Julia, and Derek Parker. *Parker's Astrology.* New York: DK Publishing, 1991.

Rogers-Gallagher, Kim. *Astrology for the Light Side of the Brain.* San Diego: ACS Publications, 1995.

Shaw, Maria. *The Enchanted Soul.* New Orleans, La.: Mid Summer's Eve Publishing, 2002.

———. *Heart and Soul.* Mt. Morris, Mich.: Mid Summer's Eve Publishing, 2001.

INDEX

Teen Goddess
How to Look, Love & Live Like a Goddess

CATHERINE WISHART

Every girl is a goddess! When you access your goddess power, you can make your life exactly as you want it to be. This positive and hip guide to beauty and spirituality will show you how—with simple messages and tasks that will illuminate your mind, body, and soul.

Remarkable things will happen when you begin to delve into your divine beauty and listen to the inner voice of the Goddess. Find romance, ace exams, radiate confidence. Enchant everybody with your appearance and your attitude. All the glamour, strength, and magic that was available to the ancient goddesses is available to you now.

0-7387-0392-3
7½ x 9⅛, 408 pp.

$14.95

To order, call 1-877-NEW-WRLD
Prices subject to change without notice

Blue Is for Nightmares

LAURIE FARIA STOLARZ

Sixteen-year-old Stacey Brown isn't the most popular girl at her boarding school, or the prettiest, or the smartest. She has confidence issues, a crush on the boyfriend of her best friend Drea, and she has painful secrets. Stacey is also a hereditary Witch.

Now she's having nightmares that someone is out to murder Drea.

Stacey feels guilty because a series of dreams several years earlier predicted a death she couldn't prevent. Now she is determined to use her skills (including folk magick, dream magick, and contacting her grandmother's ghost) to find the killer before the killer finds Drea.

Edgy and engaging, Laurie Faria Stolarz takes her readers on an unforgettable ride with this witchy thriller.

0-7387-0391-5
5³⁄₁₆ x 8, 288 pp. $8.95

To order, call 1-877-NEW-WRLD

Prices subject to change without notice

AlternaGyrl™ Horoscopes 2004

Meet AlternaGyrl™. She's feisty, funky, and wicked smart. The coming year is a never-ending astro adventure as she skips through the zodiac, bringing you monthly horoscopes and fun facts about each sign.

- Horoscopes by Maria Shaw, whirlwind public figure and author of *Maria Shaw's Star Gazer*
- Original artwork by Mister Reusch
- Shows your luckiest days of the month, major holidays, and Moon phases

0-7387-0386-9
Wall calendar, 24 pp., 12" x 12", 12 full-color paintings $12.95

Black Velvet Tarot Bag

Use this beautifully plush bag to carry and protect any of your treasured Oracles: tarot cards, runes and rune cards, Tattwa cards, and more. Sized to fit large and small decks.

0-7387-0208-0
100 percent cotton velvet with purple satin lining and matching drawstring and tassels

$12.95

WE'D LOVE TO HEAR FROM YOU...

GOT IDEAS?

Llewellyn would love to know what kinds of books you are looking for but can't seem to find. What do you want to know about? What types of books will speak specifically to you? What New Age subject areas do you feel need to be covered? If you have ideas, suggestions, or comments, write to Megan at:

megana@llewellyn.com

Llewellyn Publications
Attn: Megan, Acquisitions
P.O. Box 64383-0383
St. Paul, MN 55164-0383
USA

1-800-THE MOON (1-800-843-6666)

TO WRITE TO THE AUTHOR

If you wish to contact the author or would like
more information about this book, please write
to the author in care of Llewellyn Worldwide
and we will forward your request. Both the author
and publisher appreciate hearing from you and learning of
your enjoyment of this book and how it has helped you. Llewellyn
Worldwide cannot guarantee that every letter written to the author
can be answered, but all will be forwarded. Please write to:

Maria Shaw
% Llewellyn Worldwide
P.O. Box 64383, Dept. 0-7387-0422-9
St. Paul, MN 55164-0383, U.S.A.

Please enclose a self-addressed stamped envelope for reply,
or $1.00 to cover costs. If outside U.S.A., enclose
international postal reply coupon.

Many of Llewellyn's authors have websites with additional information and resources. For more information, please visit our website
at http://www.llewellyn.com